*Practical Manual of
Site Development*

Practical Manual of Site Development

B. C. Colley

McGraw-Hill Book Company

New York • St. Louis • San Francisco • Auckland • Bogotá • Hamburg
Johannesburg • London • Madrid • Mexico • Montreal • New Delhi
Panama • Paris • São Paulo • Singapore • Sydney • Tokyo • Toronto

Library of Congress Cataloging in Publication Data

Colley, B. C.
  Practical manual of site development

  Includes index.
 1. Civil engineering—Handbooks, manuals, etc.
2. Building sites—Handbooks, manuals, etc.   3. City
planning—Handbooks, manuals, etc.   I. Title.
TA151.C65   1985   624   84-26189
ISBN 0-07-011803-5

 234567890 KGP/KGP 89876

ISBN 0-07-011803-5

The editors for this book were Rita Margolies and Joan Zseleczky, the
designer was Jules Perlmutter, and the production supervisor was Thomas G.
Kowalczyk. It was set in Century Schoolbook by University Graphics, Inc.

Printed and bound by The Kingsport Press.

In memory of my father
Irvin S. Duncan
who often told me,
"Complications are just misarrangements of simplifications."

ABOUT THE AUTHOR

B. C. Colley is a licensed civil engineer working as a private consultant in San Jose, California. A graduate of the University of California at Davis, Colley specialized in land development engineering, focusing on such areas as hydrology and hydraulic systems design, solid and waterborne waste, natural resources and environmental impact, geology, political science, and transportation studies. Prior to entering the university, practical experience was acquired as a highway engineering technician and as a designer of custom homes.

Contents

List of Illustrations

List of Tables

Equations

2-1 $\cos 50° = \dfrac{\overline{AC}}{\overline{AB}}$

2-2 $\sin 50° = \dfrac{\overline{CB}}{\overline{AB}}$

5-1 $V_R = \dfrac{V}{1.00 - S}$

5-2 $V = \dfrac{(A_1 + A_2)}{2} L$

6-1 $L = \dfrac{\Delta}{360°} 2\pi R$

6-2 $T = R \tan \dfrac{\Delta}{2}$

6-3 $\overline{DB} = 2\left(R \sin \dfrac{\Delta}{2}\right)$

6-4 $\overline{AC} = \dfrac{R}{\cos \dfrac{\Delta}{2}}$

6-5 $\overline{CF} = \dfrac{R}{\cos \dfrac{\Delta}{2}} - R$

6-6 $\overline{EF} = R - R \cos \dfrac{\Delta}{2}$

6-7 $\overline{AE} = R \cos \dfrac{\Delta}{2}$

6-8 $K = \dfrac{L_{CL}}{R_{CL}}$

6-9 $K = \dfrac{L_{CRB}}{R_{CRB}}$

6-10 $L_{CRB} = K \times R_{CRB}$

6-11 $m = \dfrac{(G_1 - G_2)L}{8}$

6-12 $d = \dfrac{\chi^2(G_1 - G_2)}{2L}$

6-13 $\chi_c = \dfrac{LG_1}{G_1 - G_2}$

7-1 $Q = VA$ (continuity equation)

7-2 $A = \pi r^2$

7-3 $D = \left(\dfrac{4A}{\pi}\right)^{1/2}$

7-4 $A_R = \dfrac{Q}{V}$

7-5 $V = \dfrac{1.49}{n} R_H{}^{2/3} S^{1/2}$ (Manning's equation)

7-6 $R_H = \dfrac{a}{p}$ (hydraulic radius)

7-7 $R_H = \dfrac{D}{4}$

7-8 $K = \dfrac{L}{R} = \dfrac{L_{ss}}{R_{ss}}$

7-9 $L_{ss} = K \times R_{ss}$

8-1 $Q = CIA$ (rational formula)

8-2 $A_R = \dfrac{Q}{V}$

8-3 $V = \dfrac{1.486}{n} R_H{}^{2/3} S^{1/2}$ (Manning's equation)

8-4 $t = \dfrac{l}{60\,V}$

Examples

Preface

Until now, there has been no comprehensive reference source for the engineers and paraprofessionals involved in the civil engineering design of land development projects. Though there are many textbooks on specific aspects of civil engineering related to land development, they delve deeply into the theory of their subject and require an understanding of higher mathematics and physics. These textbooks are valuable for education and reference but are cumbersome for day-to-day guidance and referral. The need for a practical handbook that presents an overview is apparent. This handbook fills that need while presenting political, economic, and construction considerations as well as physical limitations. The interrelationships between the design of each aspect and every other aspect are presented in this book so that all functions are coordinated to result in a project that can be practically implemented.

Engineering students leave college or university with a diploma in hand and their formal education behind them, but their training is still ahead. The *Practical Manual of Site Development* will be their guidebook to that training as well as a daily reference. It will save immeasurable time otherwise spent leafing through textbooks, past pages of esoteric information, to find one simple formula.

Many engineers spend a great deal of time inefficiently doing simple, repetitious tasks that could be done by technicians. But few technicians are available so engineers must either do this work themselves or take time to train junior engineers or willing drafters. Not only is this inefficient, but it is often frustrating for engineer and student alike.

Written in simple, straightforward language, the material presented in this handbook is easy for the novice to understand and utilize. Whenever technical jargon is used, it is defined. It would be an excellent choice for use as a textbook to train technicians in junior colleges, engineering offices, or technical schools. Architects, planners, and developers will find it helpful for understanding the various factors engineers must consider and problems they must solve.

References are provided at the ends of chapters for those wanting to study the subject more deeply. Listings of figures, equations, tables, and examples precede the text. Conversion tables, useful trigonometry, and useful geometry are in the appendix as well as a glossary of over 160 words.

I wish to express my appreciation to Dr. George Tchobanoglous for reading Chapters 3 and 8 of the original submittal. His suggestions and direction have helped make this book possible. I am also grateful to Richard L. Foster, L.S., David C. Freyer, P.E., Christina M. Robinson, P.E., and Wayne S. Warren for reading portions of this book and sharing their observations and suggestions with me.

B. C. Colley, R.C.E.

Chapter One

Land Development

Making the environment more useful and comfortable for humanity is the purpose of land development. Land development includes the design and construction of streets and highways; flood control facilities; potable water supply facilities; collection and treatment facilities for solid and waterborne waste products; electrical, gas, and communications facilities and buildings.

Implementing the development and improvement of land involves political, economic, and aesthetic considerations as well as engineering realities. The people involved in the project will be entrepreneurs, financiers, politicians, public agents, architects, environmentalists, building contractors, land surveyors, and engineers. Effective communication among them is essential. Lack of clear communication can be the greatest obstacle to timely, satisfactory completion of any project. The intent of this book is to present a clear description of the engineering tasks and to promote a better understanding among the various people involved in land development.

USING THIS BOOK

The engineering design of public works and private projects should be done under the supervision of a highly educated, experienced engineer. But much of the day-to-day work can be done by junior engineers and technicians. This book has been written as a guide to the engineering design of small land development projects. It should not be used for design of highways, aqueducts, flood control projects, or other large private or public works projects. Though many of the principles and techniques are the same, larger projects can be far more complicated and require more specialized expertise.

The information in this book is necessarily presented in a broad but shallow way. If you desire more depth of understanding, refer to the list of books following each chapter for further reading on the subject.

Work through each of the examples presented in the chapters. By solving these problems you will clarify the text and be more likely to retain the lessons. The examples also contain information about techniques and procedures not described in the text. A listing of figures, examples, and equations is included following the table of contents for easy retrieval and use. As you read through this book, put index tabs on pages that contain information you expect to use often.

Nomenclature

The terms "jurisdiction" and "agency" are used frequently and interchangeably throughout this book. These terms refer to the political body which has power of approval over the aspect of the design being discussed. The definition of the terms can be as diverse as participants in a town meeting or representatives of the federal goverment. The terms "pipe," "conduit," "main," and "sewer" are also used interchangeably. The use of terms varies in different parts of the country in describing governing agencies, construction materials and techniques, or maps and plans. The usage in this book should make the meaning clear. Great care has been taken to define terms and jargon when first used. However, when the meaning of a word used is not clear, then refer to the glossary.

Local Customs and Resources

The words chosen to describe various materials or procedures in this book may vary from the terms used for the same material or procedures in another part of this country or another country. It is best to use what is customary locally— unless there is clear evidence that some new terminology, material, or technique is superior. There are always those who resist change, and change initially requires additional time.

Specifications for materials were purposely avoided in writing this book. Local agencies should be consulted for design criteria and specifications. When local agencies have not established criteria, nearby agencies with similar conditions and history should be consulted. This book is written as a guide only— not as a set of rules.

Coordination

Each aspect of the improvement of any site must be coordinated with every other aspect. One may design the sanitary sewer with no problems only to discover that its location creates a problem in the design of the storm sewer. After both have been redesigned, it may be discovered that the new design creates a problem in a third area. The engineering may go smoothly only to have the client or a public agency request redesign. The plans must be polished and repolished before they will be finished.

No subject or chapter in this book should be used without the others. Each chapter necessarily focuses on one aspect of the improvements, but all aspects are inextricably tied together.

PUBLIC AGENCIES

Every project requires acquisition of permits from public agencies charged with protecting the health and welfare of the public. The agencies have established certain criteria and standards. Ordinances have been written and established as law by political processes. Failure to get approvals can mean dismantling structures and/or financial penalties. It is right and necessary for public agents to examine plans and to require changes deemed necessary.

The Role of the Public Agent

The public agents have a different perspective than the developer and engineer. They see not only the project but its impact on the immediate neighbors and the community at large. The project will affect traffic volumes and traffic flows. The region must be protected from disturbance of ecosystems. Air, noise, and water pollution must be prevented. The agencies are responsible for seeing that the sewer treatment facilities are adequate, that the project is not situated where it will be endangered by floodwaters or landslides, and that the existing or planned flood control facilities will be adequate to handle the increase in storm water runoff.

Dealing with Public Agents

It is important to establish a rapport of mutual cooperation and respect with public agents whether they be the mayor of a metropolitan area or a file clerk in the county recorder's office. We are dependent on these people for their approvals and assistance.

File clerks may have more valuable information in their heads than in all the microfiche and computers in the office. A file clerk who has been responsible for maps for many years can be worth her or his weight in gold. Very old maps and plans may be impossible to find without people like these.

The truism that your contacts are essential to success is demonstrated daily in this business. Always introduce yourself to agents and tell them whom you represent. Presentation of your card will help them remember you. Be courteous and respectful, and you will be remembered. Write down the names and positions of those you meet. Once acquaintance is established, even if just through telephone contact, information will be forthcoming more easily and quickly.

If an agency plans to deny a permit for your project, ask about their concerns. Try to come up with a solution that meets their concerns and satisfies the spirit and intent of the criteria.

ENGINEERING

There is a popular saying among civil engineers that "when alligators are snapping at your ass, you forget that you set out to drain the swamp." The private sector of land development is one of the most time-sensitive businesses. The pressure to perform multiple tasks quickly can lead to oversights and mistakes. On any given day you may work on several different jobs. Interruptions for phone calls to solve minor problems or major crises on other jobs make continuity of thought on your primary task difficult. Keep in mind what you set out to do.

There is considerable risk, particularly to young engineers, of over-engineering simple problems. Do not be seduced by precise numbers, computer printouts, and complicated solutions. Be alert to this risk and frequently check plans and results with common sense. Keep the work simple but complete.

Numbers

Two words that engineers should have a clear understanding of are "accuracy" and "precision." Accuracy refers to correctness. An answer is accurate (correct) or it is wrong. Precision is a matter of degree. An accurate measurement of 10 ft does not tell you the degree of precision. The number 10.01 is precise to within 1/100 ft. The measurement is greater than 10.00 ft but not as great as 10.02 ft. If a more precise measurement is needed, the measurement must be made to within 1/1000 or 1/10,000, and so on. A number can be accurate and not be precise. An accurate value of a slope for drainage purposes of 1 percent may be just as useful as the more precise value of 1.03 percent. But a number that is not accurate, though it may be precise, is worthless.

Your work must always be accurate. The degree of precision you select should be based on common sense. If you are designing a grading plan, 0.1 ft is sufficiently precise. The contractor will not be able to build it closer. For dimensions and elevations of structures use 0.01 ft. The degree of precision that can be accomplished may be plus or minus 0.05 ft, but do not round off or the precision will be 0.05 plus the amount rounded off.

Surveying property lines and subdivision maps requires more precision. The degree of precision depends upon the size of the parcel being surveyed. When measuring angles, 1 degree of difference results in 1.74 ft of offset difference for every 100 ft; 1 minute difference yields 0.029 ft of offset difference for every 100 ft; 1 second difference yields 0.0048 ft of offset difference for every 100 ft. The degree of precision chosen should be based on the distance measured and the precision required for the finished traverse.

In mathematical calculations, there is no advantage in using more significant figures than are found in the number in the equation which has the least number of significant figures. For example, where the circumference of a circle ($C = \pi d$) is needed and the diameter is given as 50.25 ft (four significant figures), there is no point in using more significant figures for the value of pi. Use 3.142 rather than 3.14159265. Any numbers to the right of the first four in the answer are meaningless. Keep this in mind when selecting the number of significant figures to use when making calculations. If the answer should be precise to 0.01 ft and the answer expected will be between 10 and 99 ft, four significant figures will be needed for each value used. The significant numbers can be zeros on the end of the number if zeros are an accurate representation of the degree of precision.

When you prepare preliminary cost estimates, the quantities of materials should be rounded off to no less than tens of linear feet or 100 ft^2. If the estimate is for a large project, the quantities should be rounded even further. The use of more than four or five significant figures when making an estimate which will total in the millions of dollars is senseless and misleading. When you list quantities for proposals, however, the numbers should be more precise. Once the design is complete, the exact number of linear feet of curb and square feet of paving will be known and should be used.

"Order of magnitude" is a term frequently heard in engineering. The term refers to the relative size of a number. When you have calculated an answer, check if the order of magnitude seems correct. For instance, when using the rational equation $Q = CIA$ (Eq. 8-1) and the values are $C = 0.9$, $I = 2.2$ in/h, $A = 53.1$ acres, the answer should be roughly 100 cfs ($Q \approx 1 \times 2 \times 50$). An answer close to 1000 or close to 10 is obviously wrong—it has the wrong order of magnitude.

One technique to aid in making correct calculations is to always show the dimensions of the numbers being used. Calculating numbers without showing their dimensions can lead to errors of conversion. The dimensions must be calculated as well as the numbers. Feet times feet yields square feet—area. Square feet times feet yields cubic feet—volume. If the dimension of your answer is feet to the fourth power, it is wrong, since feet to the fourth power is meaningless. When using the rational equation, $Q = CIA$ (Eq. 8-1), C is without dimension, I is given in inches per hour, and A is given in acres. If you label each value with the correct dimensions, the conversion factors needed to yield the quantity (Q) in cubic feet per second becomes apparent.

$$Q = C \times I\frac{\text{in}}{\text{h}} \times \frac{\text{h}}{3600 \text{ s}} \times \frac{\text{ft}}{12 \text{ in}} \times A \text{ acres} \frac{43,560 \text{ ft}^2}{\text{acres}} = 1.008 \, (CIA) \text{ cfs}$$

Computers

There are situations where the use of computers is clearly indicated. Once computer skills are mastered, complicated computations can be made more easily, more quickly, and with less risk of error. But, guard against becoming computer-dependent. With a little practice, simple computations can be done faster in your head. Do not be misled into believing that answers which are more precise are more accurate or more valuable. Flashing lights, electronic beeps, and computer printouts can be very impressive, but remember, the answers are only as accurate as the data fed in by computer operator.

Drawings

Drawings and sketches are an important tool for engineers. A drawing made to scale is sometimes the fastest way to find the answer to a problem. The uses of scale drawings are illustrated throughout this book. When there is an error in a traverse, plotting the coordinate points and connecting them will make the location of the error apparent. Plotting the points of a profile at a vertical scale 10 times as large as the horizontal scale clearly shows the location of any points that do not fit in a straight line or along a smooth curve.

   Members of planning commissions, city councils, and the public are seldom familiar with drawings made with exaggerated scales. Such drawings may confuse them and cause negative feelings about what you are trying to illustrate. If such drawings are necessary, precede and follow them with drawings of the same situation drawn at a natural scale where the horizontal and vertical scale are the same.

THE PROJECT

Each project is different from every other project. What is important to one developer may not be important to another. One developer may study every detail and know exactly what materials to use and how the site should drain. Another developer may want to take the most economical approach possible. Ask what approach the client wants. The most professionally designed project will not guarantee further work from that client if it is not what the client had in mind. Of course, if what the client wants would not represent good engineering practice, the developer must be educated and directed to a more acceptable approach.

Existing Conditions

It is essential that the project engineer visit the site as early in the development as possible. Each person visiting a site sees different things. It may be necessary to visit the site many times as the design progresses.

Never accept the elevations and locations of significant existing structures from previously prepared plans without having a survey crew field-check the information. During construction, differences will become apparent and the cost of redesign or reconstruction at that late stage is not worth the risk.

Criteria

The criteria established by the various jurisdictional agencies must be followed. They may be documented in several ways including standard plans and specifications and city ordinances. During the approval process, each agency involved can stipulate conditions of approval. The client will have criteria to be met, and your employer may have established criteria in the form of company policies. Other consultants, architects, traffic engineers, soils engineers, and environmentalists impose criteria as well. These criteria should be kept in mind. A list should be made and frequently checked if a project is complicated.

Building Setback Requirements

Planning criteria affect all sites. It is imperative for the engineer to calculate the required building setback distances. Whether the building is residential, commercial, or industrial, there will be a minimum distance required between the building and the property lines. Buildings must also be located clear of easements. *Easements* are rights of limited usage held by one owner over the property of another owner. Plot easements affecting the site, and read the intent and restrictions imposed by them. Clearance of the easements must also be verified. Overhangs and patios may be described separately with setbacks to be used.

Lot and building sizes are sometimes the result of these setback distances. If several different house plans are planned for a particular subdivision, the engineer may be asked to prepare a "fit list" of which house plans fit which lots. On lots where the fit is questionable, the clearances can be calculated, but this can be a time-consuming process. Another approach is to carefully draw a simplified drawing at a large scale and measure the setback distances.

The setback distances on commercial and industrial sites should be calculated at all critical points. This should be done before design of other improvements is begun. The architect or planner will have plotted the buildings on a drawing of the property taken from the deed. When the deed is analyzed by the surveyor and a field investigation of the boundary is complete, the distances and bearings may be different from the deed. When the distances between building and property line are less than required for setbacks, the client and/ or architect should be informed immediately, as the design of the building will have to be altered to comply with the setback requirements.

Timing

The statement "time is money" was never more true than in the land development business. When the economy is booming, land development and construction are booming. The faster the projects can be built, the more money can be made. When economic growth is slow, many developers are forced out of business. In fast-growing areas, the political and financial situation can change quickly. The various fees for building permits or sewer connections can be doubled or tripled with very little warning. Building moratoriums prohibiting further development can be imposed at any time. In most areas, wet weather limits the months suitable for construction. These are some of the reasons why developers often expect the engineering design to be done quickly. Do not let the time constraints cause you to be careless or to leave out important checking.

Ideally the topography and boundary survey will be complete before the tentative map is drawn, and the tentative map approvals will be complete before the parcel or final maps are begun. What sometimes happens, however, is that all these processes are started with the signing of the contract. The planners start drawing a tentative map from the deed, and calculations are started for a final map. The surveyors are sent into the field for boundary and topography, and drafters begin work on base maps for the engineering design.

Once these tasks are under way, the engineer gathers information on the design of existing and proposed utilities in the area. A visit to the site is essential to spot potential trouble spots in the topography. An estimate of the existing elevations may be made from previous projects in the area, topography of adjacent projects, or U.S. Geological Survey Maps.

There are many risks in starting the engineering tasks simultaneously. Existing streets and utilities are seldom constructed exactly as designed. As-built plans are not positively representative of elevations and locations. The condition for approval of the tentative map may require facilities not planned for, and field investigation of the boundary may reveal that there is less available land than needed. The true topography may be quite different than anticipated. These differences must be corrected on the plans, adjustments made, and the deadline still met. Any time changes are made, the potential for error is greatly increased. Utmost care must be exercised to follow through on every aspect of the design affected by changes.

Errors and Omissions

Delays during construction to solve engineering problems are very costly. The solution to a problem that becomes apparent during construction is often the removal and replacement of new structures—obviously an expensive procedure. Equipment and personnel standing idle while the problem is solved can cost thousands of dollars per hour. The funds for construction are often borrowed, and delays in completion may result in interest charges of thousands of dollars a day.

Thoroughness in research of existing and proposed facilities is essential. Often when design is in progress for one lot or one tract, design also will be in progress for adjacent or nearby property. Remember to ask public agents about other projects in the area. Their design and state of completion may impact your project.

If the engineer's oversight costs the clients money, you can be sure that they will look elsewhere for an engineer for their next project, or they will look to this engineer for compensation.

Chapter Two

Maps and Plans

This chapter will describe the types of maps and plans engineers use. Confusion results when these terms are used interchangeably. The two are different. Though maps are sometimes used to illustrate plans for orderly development, engineering plans are not used as maps. The terms will be defined and the differences clarified in this chapter.

MAPS

Drawings that show the relative locations of various aspects of the physical and legal environment are called *maps*. Maps are usually two dimensional and show only horizontal relationships. Relief maps are three dimensional and illustrate the highs and lows of the ground level. Only two-dimensional maps will be discussed in this book.

Topography maps show physical environments. Topography is included on some of the other maps discussed in this chapter. Boundary survey maps and subdivision maps serve as legal descriptions and locate parcels of land exactly and to the exclusion of the rest of the world.

Maps as Resources

Modern land development would be impossible without maps. Street maps, assessor's maps, zoning maps, flood zone insurance maps, fault zone maps, U.S. Geological Survey (USGS) maps, and assessment district maps are some of the kinds of maps used by engineers involved in land development.

Street Maps

When the word "map" is used, most people think of a street or road map. We all have had the experience of using these maps. They are essential when traveling in unfamiliar areas. Street and road maps can be purchased at a gas station or acquired at city and county offices or chamber of commerce offices. Automobile clubs such as the Automobile Association of America (AAA) have excellent street and road maps. Street maps can also be purchased at stationery, grocery, and drug stores.

Assessor's Maps

One of the first sources of information the engineer uses is assessor's maps (Fig. 2-1). Assessor's maps are used to locate property for the purpose of taxation and contain much useful information. These maps are available in the assessor's or tax collector's offices.

If one knows cross streets near the site, the book where the map of the property is located can be determined from an index map. Within this book is another index map to help locate the map (page) that actually shows the property. The page is delineated with the various property lines, and each property

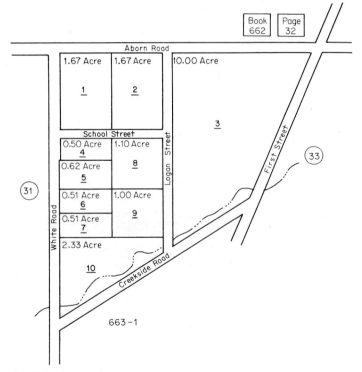

Fig. 2-1   Assessor's map.

Fig. 2-2 Zoning map. *(Courtesy of the county of Santa Clara, CA.)*

RESOURCE CONSERVATION AREAS

Baylands

Agriculture – Large Scale

Agriculture – Medium Scale

Hillsides

Ranchlands

Open Space Reserve (---temporary boundary)

Existing Regional Parks

Other Public Open Lands

RURAL RESIDENTIAL AREAS

OTHER LAND USES

Areas with Special Land Use Policies

Major Educational & Institutional Uses

Major Public Facilities

Communication and Utilities

Transportation

Roadside Services

• Active Solid Waste Disposal Sites, 1980
o Past Solid Waste Disposal Sites

Industrial Facilities

Quarries (not yet delineated)

URBAN SERVICE AREA

LIMIT OF FUTURE URBAN EXPANSION (not yet delineated)

NOTE:
Proposed Parks are Shown on the Regional Parks, Trails and Scenic Highways Map
This map includes changes in public ownership designations
or reflect acquisitions to 6/15/81 and corrections to earlier maps.

APPLICABILITY

13

is given a lot number. Each property on the tax rolls is identified with a number representing book-page-lot such as 662-32-3 (Fig. 2-1). The number is then listed in another book where the name and address of the owner and the assessed valuation of the property are given. Reference is given at the edges of the page to show which book and page shows the adjacent properties.

Other information is shown on assessor's maps. The names and file numbers of existing subdivisions and Record of Survey maps in the area may be given. Distances along property lines may be shown but are not legal dimensions and should be used only as approximations. Street names and widths may be shown as well as some easements and rights-of-way. The information on the assessor's map provides a useful sketch for following the legal description. It is of a scale and size that is easily carried and referred to. It also provides a map that can be given to the surveyors and other consultants working on the project in the early stages of development. With the reference numbers for subdivisions and Records of Surveys adjacent to the site, existing improvement or construction plans can be located.

Zoning Maps

The purpose of zoning maps is to show zoning districts (Fig. 2-2). The districts are used to control population densities and the character of growth. The intent is to have compatible land uses adjacent and incompatible uses separate. The types of zones are industrial, commercial, business and professional, and residential. The zones are further subdivided to refine densities and uses. The sizes of lots and required building setback distances for specific zones are described in city ordinances. Before work is begun, compliance of the project with zoning requirements must be verified.

Deviation from existing zoning can sometimes be allowed through political process. This usually requires a significant amount of time. "Planned developments" (not to be confused with development plans) can sometimes circumvent specific ordinance requirements if the developer can demonstrate that there is good cause and that the essence of the zoning is upheld. There is experimentation in some areas with mixed use zoning, wherein commercial, business-professional, and residential uses are placed together (Fig. 2-3).

U.S. Geological Survey Maps

In the early stages of research for a project, USGS maps can be useful. These maps are topographic maps showing large areas (Fig. 2-4). Because of the scale, only the general topography can be shown. That is, areas are shown as occupied generally by buildings or orchards or open fields. This information may be outdated, but the maps show contours, and, in lieu of having more specific information, the maps will provide the direction of the slope of the land. Other information such as the existence of a well on the site may also be shown.

Fig. 2-3 Example of mixed use zoning in Palo Alto, California. A restaurant, retail shops, and offices are on the street floor. Offices are on the second floor. Residential apartments are on the third and fourth floors. *(Courtesy of Crosby, Thornton, Marshall Associates Architects, San Francisco, CA. Project Architect, Lynn Yandell, AIA.)*

Locating Land

Before construction can begin, a clear and exact location of the property boundary must be established. The deed is the legal description of the property. Its interpretation should be made by a qualified licensed land surveyor or an engineer experienced in interpretation of property descriptions. In the simplest cases a legal description of a property will be, for example, "Lot 1, Tract 5200, filed February 26, 1969, in Book 323 of Maps, at page 65, Santa Clara County Records." But, in most cases, the legal description is more complicated and may continue for pages describing the property by "metes and bounds" (explained below). If a subdivision map or monuments were used in the legal description of the property, a surveyor will have to establish their physical locations. Usually monuments are set at subdivision and lot or parcel corners. Monuments can be anything described by the deed. They can be anything from charcoal buried at the property corner to the cornerstone of a skyscraper. Commonly ¾-in IPs (iron pipes) tagged with the surveyor's or engineer's license number are installed along subdivision boundaries.

The following are some of the kinds of elements used in land descriptions:

1. *Subdivision maps.* The "southerly corner of Lot 1, as shown on that certain map entitled, 'Map of W. E. Woodhams Subdivision.'"
2. *Streets.* "Beginning at the point of intersection of the northwesterly line of Alum Rock Avenue (100 feet wide) with the northeasterly line of Jackson Avenue (60 feet wide)."
3. *Other deeds.* "Beginning at the most southerly corner of that parcel of land described in the deed from Henry W. Smith, *et ux,*[1] to George Davis,

---

[1]*Et ux* is an abbreviation of Latin for "and wife," *et vir* for "and husband," and *et al* for "and others."

16

Fig. 2-4 U.S. Geological Survey Map.

17

et ux, dated December 10, 1954, and recorded December 15, 1954, in Book 303 of Official Records, page 288, Sonoma County Records."

    4. *Monuments.* "From a ¾-in IP at the southerly corner of Tract 5200 . . ."

Metes and Bounds

Property is often established with a metes and bounds description. The term "metes and bounds" is an all-inclusive description. "Bounds" can be anything that limits the parcel of land to be described.

    Often a property description begins from a locatable point and traverses the property with bearings and distances. Bearings are directions as measured east or west of north or south. They must be exact, and so are measured in degrees, minutes, seconds, and decimals of a second and are determined in the following way. A circle is divided into 360°.[2] Each degree is divided into 60 minutes (minutes are abbreviated ′) and each minute into 60 seconds (seconds are abbreviated ″). The course is described as a certain number of degrees, minutes, and seconds (from 0° to 90°) east or west of north, or a certain number of degrees, minutes, and seconds east or west of south. A line described as N50°E can also be described as S50°W. The direction of the course determines whether the bearing is northeast or southwest (Fig. 2-5). In a metes and bounds description, the bearings and distances serve to traverse property. The following is an example of the metes and bounds description of the property in Fig. 2-6.

All that certain real property situate in the City of Redding, County of Shasta, State of California, described as follows:

Beginning at the point of intersection of the Northerly line of Main Street, 50 feet wide, and the Easterly line of First Street, 40 feet wide; thence along said Easterly

[2]The metric system divides circles into 400 increments. Each increment is called a grad.

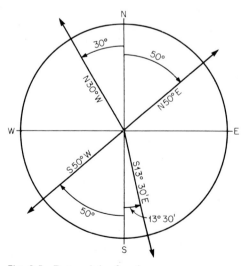

Fig. 2-5 Determining bearings.

line of First Street N5°22′36″E, 201.50 feet to the Southerly boundary of Tract 5700, filed March 4, 1965, in Book 376 of Maps, at page 31, Shasta County Records; thence along the said Southerly boundary of said Tract 5700, N89°52′22″E, 247.13 feet to the Westerly line of Second Street, 60 feet wide; thence along Second Street S5°22′36″W, 170.98 feet; thence along a curve to the right with a radius of 30.00 feet, through a central angel of 83°40′32″ an arc length of 43.81 feet to a point on the Northerly line of Main Street; thence S89°03′08″W, 220.66 feet to the Point of Beginning.

Containing 1.12 acres more or less.

Accurate interpretation or writing of metes and bounds descriptions is an exacting skill beyond the scope of this book. If more information on this subject is desired, refer to the book *Land Survey Descriptions* by William C. Wattles.

Townships and Sections

The first method used to establish property lines was that of metes and bounds description; however, much of the United States was surveyed by U.S. government surveyors and divided into townships. Establishment of townships and sections is a complicated procedure beyond the scope of this book. An idealization of the procedure is provided here.

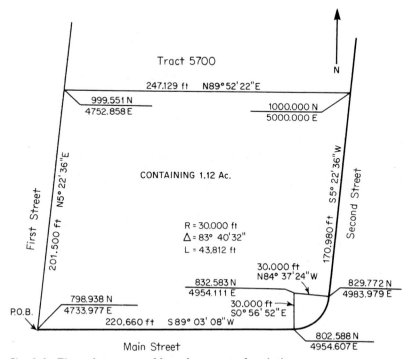

Fig. 2-6 Figure for metes and bounds property description.

The establishment of townships is based on the latitudes and longitudes of the earth. *Longitudes* are imaginary lines running north and south through the poles. Each longitude is identified as from 0° to 180° east or west of Greenwich, England. *Latitudes* are lines extending around the earth, parallel to the equator and divided in degrees, from 0° at the equator to 90° at the poles.

Prominent local geographical points are identified by latitude and longitude, and then referred to for further refinement. Mt. Diablo in Northern California is at latitude 37°51′30″N and longitude 121°54′48″W. It is the reference point in descriptions using "Mt. Diablo Base and Meridian." There are two other base and meridian points in California—San Bernardino Base and Meridian, and Humbolt Base and Meridian.

From these base (latitude) and meridian (longitude) lines, townships are established. *Townships* are rectangular blocks of land 6 mi square. They are described by their distance from the base and meridian. The land contained in the first 6 mi north of the base line is said to be in Township 1 North. The land within the first 6 mi south is said to be in Township 1 South. The land contained in the second 6 mi north is Township 2 North, and so on. The east and west limits of the township are measured in 6-mi increments east and west and referred to as ranges. The township and range terms are abbreviated. T5N, R2E, MDB&M (Township 5 North, Range 2 East, Mt. Diablo Base and Meridian) is illustrated in Fig. 2-7. The township is further divided into "sections" of land approximately 1 mi square containing approximately 640 acres. The sections are numbered from 1 to 36 starting at the northeasterly corner of the township and continuing back and forth across the township in a zigzag manner (Fig. 2-8).

The section is further divided into halves, and quarters, and quarter quarter sections and so on. The quarters are established by bisecting the boundaries of the section. The points of bisection are called *quarter corners*. Lines are then drawn between quarter corners to establish quarter sections. The property described as "the North half of the Northeast quarter of the Southwest quarter of section 26 T5N, R2E, MDB&M" is shown in Fig. 2-9. To interpret descriptions in this form, start reading at the end of the sentence and trace the process backward.

Example 2-1

Determine the approximate distance (in miles) between MDB&M and the west quarter corner of section 7 T5N, R2E. Use Figs. 2-7, 2-8, and 2-9.

Solution

T5N occupies the land between 24 and 30 mi north of MDB&M. Section 7 lies between 4 mi and 5 mi north of the south boundary of Township 5N. The west quarter corner is 0.5 miles north of the section corner.

$$24 \text{ mi} + 4 \text{ mi} + 0.5 \text{ mi} = 28.5 \text{ mi north of the base.}$$

R2E lies between 6 and 12 mi east of the meridian. Section 7 lies between 0 and 1 mi east of the range line; the west quarter corner is on the west line (0 mi east of the range line).

$$6 \text{ mi} + 0 \text{ mi} + 0 \text{ mi} = 6 \text{ mi east of the meridian.}$$

The west quarter corner of section 7 is 28.5 mi north and 6 mi east of MDB&M

The exact dimensions of the distances along the sides of a section (1 mi = 5280 ft) and portions of a section will vary from expected dimensions because of inaccuracies in the original surveys. Also, longitudes (meridian lines) converge from the equator to the poles. When adjustment is made for the convergence, the sections along the north and west of the township are made to accommodate the variance.

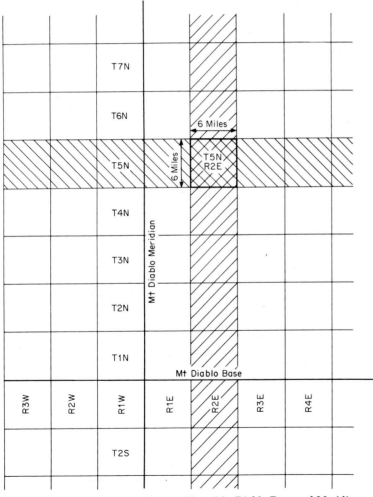

Fig. 2-7 Township 5 North, Range 2 East, Mt. Diablo Base and Meridian.

1 mile

6	5	4	3	2	1
7	8	9	10	11	12
18	17	16	15	14	13
19	20	21	22	23	24
30	29	28	27	26	25
31	32	33	34	35	36

6 miles

Fig. 2-8   Township divided into sections.

The townships were originally established by government surveyors in the late 1700s and early 1800s as a result of political persuasion by Thomas Jefferson. As a general rule, monuments were set at section corners and quarter corners. Even though the work was sometimes done under very difficult conditions

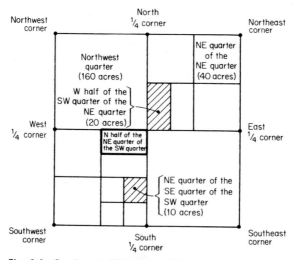

Fig. 2-9 Section 26, T5N, R2E MDB&M.

and with instruments that were crude by today's standards, the original monuments, when they can be found, hold the most credibility for determining the location of sections. The original surveys are recorded on "government plat maps," and survey (call) notes are available from Bureau of Land Management offices.

Coordinate Systems

One of the most useful tools at the engineer's disposal is coordinate systems. The importance of coordinate systems in surveying is great and gaining more extensive use with modern surveying equipment and computer-aided drafting (CAD) systems. A basic understanding of their use is desirable even though step-by-step procedures can be followed with computers to determine information without understanding the basics. A background of trigonometry and algebra is necessary for understanding coordinate systems.

Coordinates are numbers representing distances north and east of a reference point. The reference point can be real such as Mt. Diablo Base and Meridian, or it can be fictional. Coordinate systems employ trigonometric relationships between points to determine unknown distances and bearings. The use of a coordinate system also facilitates location and plotting of property corners and other survey points with accuracy and precision.

The reference point is at the point of the 90° intersection of a north-south axis with an east-west axis. The north-south axis can be assumed north, magnetic north, or true north. The point can be given coordinates based on another coordinate system to which ties are to be made or given arbitrary coordinates that are convenient to the task.

In Fig. 2-10, point A is the reference point and has been assigned coordinates of 1000.000N and 2000.000E. When traversing a course which is 500.00 ft long

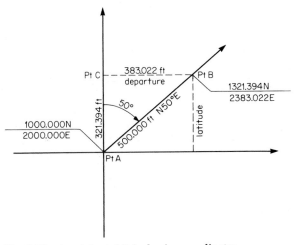

Fig. 2-10   A point established using coordinates.

on a bearing of N 50°E from point *A*, the course will end at point *B*. The difference in northerly coordinates is called the *latitude*. The difference in easterly coordinates is called the *departure*. A right triangle is formed by the course, N 50°E, 500.00 ft, the latitude measured along the north-south axis, and the departure as measured from point *C* to point *B*.

From trigonometry we know that the cosine of angle *CAB* (50°) is equal to the length of $\overline{AC}$ divided by the length of course $\overline{AB}$.

$$\cos 50° = \frac{\overline{AC}}{\overline{AB}} \tag{2-1}$$

This formula can be manipulated to yield the unknown latitude *(AC)*.

$$\begin{aligned}\overline{AC} &= \overline{AB} \times \cos 50° \\ &= 500.000 \text{ ft} \times 0.642788 \\ &= 321.394 \text{ ft}\end{aligned}$$

The northing coordinate for point *B* is

$$1000.000\text{N} + 321.394 \text{ ft} = 1321.394\text{N}$$

Trigonometry also gives us the relationship that the sine of angle *CAB* (50°) is equal to the length of $\overline{CB}$ divided by the length of course $\overline{AB}$.

$$\sin 50° = \frac{\overline{CB}}{\overline{AB}} \tag{2-2}$$

Again manipulating the formula, the departure $\overline{CB}$ can be determined.

$$\begin{aligned}\overline{CB} &= \overline{AB} \times \sin 50° \\ &= 500.000 \text{ ft} \times 0.766044 \\ &= 383.022 \text{ ft}\end{aligned}$$

The easterly coordinate for point *B* is

$$2000.000\text{E} + 383.022 \text{ ft} = 2383.022\text{E}$$

If the coordinates of points *A* and *B* are known but the distances and bearing between them are not, the course between them could be determined. The northerly coordinate of point *B* (1321.394) minus the northerly coordinate of point *A* (1000.00) gives the latitude 321.394. The easterly coordinate for point *B* (2383.022) minus the easterly coordinate of point *A* (2000.00) gives the departure 383.022 ft. From trigonometry we know that the tangent of the angle *CAB* is

$$\begin{aligned}\tan \angle CAB &= \frac{\overline{CB}}{\overline{CA}} \\ &= \frac{383.022 \text{ ft}}{321.394 \text{ ft}} = 1.19313\end{aligned}$$

The angle whose tangent is 1.19313 is 50°. To find the length of the line we again use trigonometry.

$$\sin \angle CAB = \frac{\overline{CB}}{\overline{AB}}$$

$$\overline{AB} = \frac{\overline{CB}}{\sin \angle CAB}$$

$$= \frac{383.022 \text{ ft}}{\sin 50°} = \frac{383.022 \text{ ft}}{0.766044}$$

$$= 500.000 \text{ ft}$$

A series of courses can be traversed to delineate property lines such as shown in Figure 2-6.

An illustration of how to determine coordinates for the property in Fig. 2-6 is given in Fig. 2-11. The traverse starts at assumed coordinates at the northeast corner of the property. The coordinates chosen for that point are large enough that the property will have all positive coordinates and small enough that unnecessary numbers will not have to be carried. The number for the easting coordinate was chosen with the same considerations and so that the easting coordinates would not be confused with the northing coordinates.

When a traverse contains one or two "unknowns" but the beginning and ending coordinates are known, the unknown information can be calculated. The unknowns can be:

The bearing and distance of one course as illustrated earlier. This is called inversing.

The bearings of two courses.

The distances of two courses.

The bearing of one course and the distance of another course.

Procedures for solving unknowns in two courses are long and complicated, and there are many opportunities for errors. Fortunately, hand-held calculators and computers do this task easily and quickly when simple step-by-step instruc-

Distance	Bearing	Cosine	Sine	Northing	Easting	Point
				1000.000	5000.000	1
170.980	S 5° 22' 36" W	0.995600	0.093703	− 170.228	− 16.021	
				829.772	4983.979	2
30.000	N 84° 37' 24" W			+ 2.811	− 29.868	
				832.583	4954.111	3
30.000	S 0° 56' 52" E	0.999863	0.016541	− 29.996	+ 0.496	
				802.587	4954.607	4
220.660	S 89° 03' 08" W			− 3.650	− 220.630	
				798.937	4733.977	5
201.500	N 5° 22' 36" E	0.995600	0.093703	+ 200.613	+ 18.881	
				999.550	4752.858	6
247.129	N 89° 52' 22" E	0.002220	0.999998	+ 0.549	+ 247.128	
				1000.099	4999.986	
				1000.000	5000.000	1
			Error of closure	0.099	0.014	

Fig. 2-11 Calculation of coordinates for the boundary of property in Fig. 2-6.

tions are followed. A computer printout for the traverse in Fig. 2-6 is included as Fig. 2-12.

Maps as Tools

Engineers use a variety of maps to illustrate how they will implement the improvements. Before design can begin, topography and boundary maps must be prepared. From information on them, preliminary maps are drawn. Alternative locations for streets and lot lines can be laid out for residential sites,

```
N1=1,000.0000          L=-3.6500
E1=5,000.0000          D=-220.6298

S 5.2236 W             N5=798.9375
HD=170.9800            E5=4,733.9771

L=-170.2277            N 5.2236 E
D=-16.0213             HD=201.5000

N2=829.7723            L=200.6134
E2=4,983.9787          D=18.8811

N 84.3724 W            N6=999.5510
HD=30.0000             E6=4,752.8582

L=2.8111               N 89.5222 E
D=-29.8680             HD=247.1290

N3=832.5834            L=0.5487
E3=4,954.1107          D=247.1284

S 0.5652 E             N7=1,000.0997
HD=30.0000             E7=4,999.9866

L=-29.9959             S 7.3844 E
D=0.4962               HD=0.1006

N4=802.5875            L=-0.0997
E4=4,954.6069          D=0.0134

S 89.0308 W            N8=1,000.0000
HD=220.6600            E8=5,000.0000
```

Fig. 2-12 Computer printout of the calculation of coordinates for the boundary of property in Fig. 2-6.

buildings can be placed, and parking lots can be designed for industrial and commercial sites. When several preliminary plans have been considered, one is selected and a tentative map prepared for presentation to city council meetings and other committees and agencies for approval. Once the approvals have been obtained, the final map (parcel map, tract map, or condominium map) can be prepared.

Boundary Maps

A boundary map is a drawing, made to scale, of the property lines enclosing the site. It shows the bearing and distance of each course and any monuments found or set. When the survey is performed to prepare the map, a Record of Survey map might have to be filed at the appropriate agency. In California, the office of the county surveyor for the county in which the property lies is the approving agency. The map should show identifying numbers of adjacent subdivisions and other Records of Surveys made at or near the site. Any existing easements should be shown as well.

Topography Maps

A topography map illustrates all the important physical characteristics of a site (Fig. 2-13). Anything that may affect demolition, design, or construction and anything that may have to be protected, saved, accommodated, or connected to should be shown. Their type (concrete, asphalt, brick) and condition should be noted on the map. Some items to be shown are:

Buildings
Streets and roads
Railroads, mainlines, and spurs
Sidewalks
Curbs and gutters
Trees (include type), streams, rock outcroppings
Elevations and contours (described in Chap. 5)
Electroliers, power and telephone poles
Fences and walls
Manholes, water and gas valves
Underground conduits
Wells
Underground tanks and cesspools
Easements
Flood plain zones
Earthquake fault zones

The agencies whose approvals will be needed may have a legend of symbols to use for the various topographic features. If not, the symbols should be clear and a legend should be included on the map.

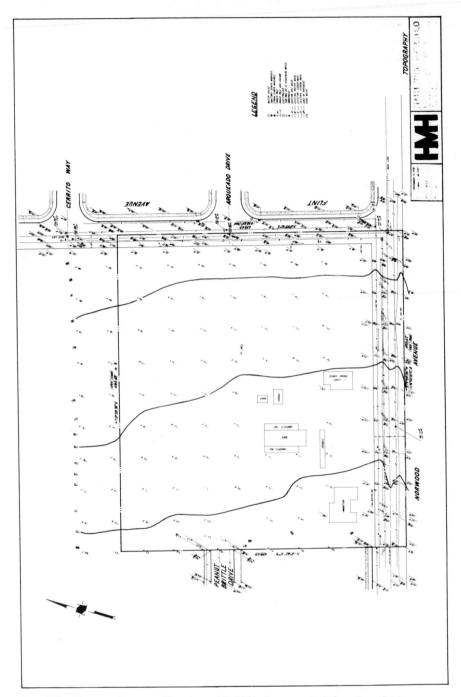

Fig. 2-13 Topography map. *(Courtesy of H.M.H., Incorporated, San Jose, CA.)*

Preliminary Maps

Ideally, boundary and topography maps should be complete when the preparation of preliminary maps is started. However, since timing is critical in land development, work on the preliminary map may precede the boundary and topography maps. When this happens, approximate boundaries are often plotted from the deed. Locations of topography that may affect the layout of the project should be plotted as closely to the correct location as possible.

Planners and architects often plot the initial layout of buildings or lots and streets. Their concerns are for such things as compliance with zoning, efficient use of the area, and aesthetics. The client may want the project to be a monument to his or her success, to have the ambience of a college campus, or, more likely, to include as many lots or as much building area as physically possible. It is the engineers' or planners' task to accommodate these criteria and the physical conditions and to present various alternative preliminary plans to the client for selection.

Attention must be directed to existing easements. If a neighbor, utility company, or other owner has the right to use a portion of the property for access to other properties or facilities, a portion of the client's property may have limited use. This is the time to verify that all the constraints on the property are acknowledged.

If the site has significant amount of slope, cut or fill slopes between the lots or building pads will be necessary. The amount of space occupied by slopes must be delineated or retaining walls must be planned so their cost will be reflected in preliminary estimates. A good deal of money may be spent on the planning and engineering of a project only to have the project redesigned if easements and slopes are not accounted for in the early stages.

Tentative Maps

When the preliminary plans are complete and one alternative is selected, a tentative map is prepared. The tentative map serves to show approving agencies what is planned. What is shown on a tentative map can be as simple as a proposed division of a lot into two parcels or as complicated as a "new town." State and local laws and ordinances determine the circumstances under which a tentative map must be prepared and which agencies will have rights of approval.

The requirement of approvals is primarily to protect public health and safety. It may be required that the map show drawings of such things as street widths, percentages of coverage of the property by buildings, streets, and landscaping; agencies supplying utilities; number of people to occupy the site; and amount of traffic generated by the project. Approving agencies can require whatever information they deem appropriate. Usually the tentative map will be approved subject to certain conditions. The conditions of approval will have to be satisfied. It is a good practice to copy the conditions of approval and attach them to the tentative map. The project engineer can then take the tentative map and conditions of approval and prepare the subdivision map and construction plans.

Subdivision Maps

A subdivision map is a legal document. Its purpose is to illustrate exact legal location and description of plots of land. The map is used in place of metes and bounds descriptions. It can take the form of a parcel map (Fig. 2-14), a tract map[3] (Fig. 2-15a and b), or a condominium map.[4] The map becomes a legal document when it has been signed by the land owner, the surveyor or qualified civil engineer, and the consenting agencies and filed for record. From that point on, property can be bought and sold by reference to that map.

Use of a parcel map has limiting criteria, for example, that no more than five lots will be created with the map and that each lot has access to a public street or highway. When more than five lots are to be created, a subdivision map must be used. The requirements for the creation of subdivision maps are spelled out by state and local laws.

PLANS

The term "plan" can refer to anything from saying "let's eat" to volumes of books and drawings describing methods and procedures to accomplish some result. In engineering and allied fields, *plans* usually refer to drawings made to scale showing horizontal, vertical, and cross-sectional views of tangible objects to be built. Plans can include written descriptions of construction procedures (specifications), artists' renderings, or any other device to help make clear what is to be accomplished.

Types of Plans

Some of the various types of plans used in land development will be briefly described in this section. It is important to remember that the nomenclature may be different in one location than in another. For instance, the plans referred to here as "construction plans" may be called "improvement plans" in your locale. Do not let that distract you. The purpose and character of the plans will be the same.

---

[3]Subdivision maps creating more than five parcels may be called tract maps, and the property may be assigned a tract number. The assignment of a tract number facilitates referencing.

[4]Condominiums provide ownership of an apartment or office "unit" (air space) with a proportionate undivided ownership of the underlying real property. The owner of a townhouse unit holds exclusive right to the underlying land, and a subdivision or tract map is used to define ownership. An undivided ownership to common areas may be held by a townhouse owner.

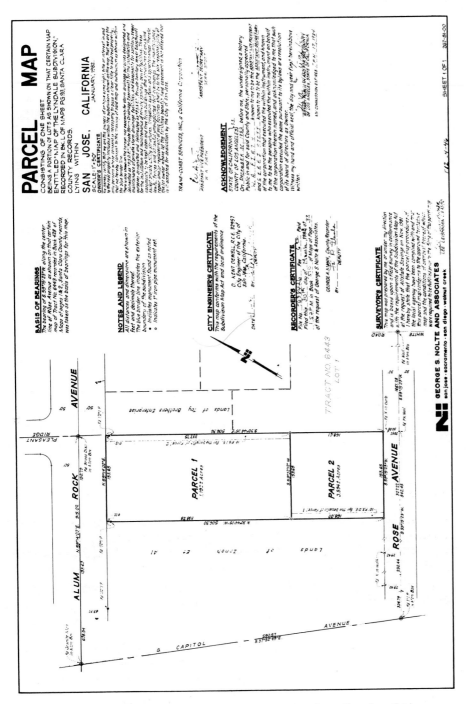

Fig. 2-14 Parcel map. *(Courtesy of George S. Nolte and Associates, San Jose, CA.)*

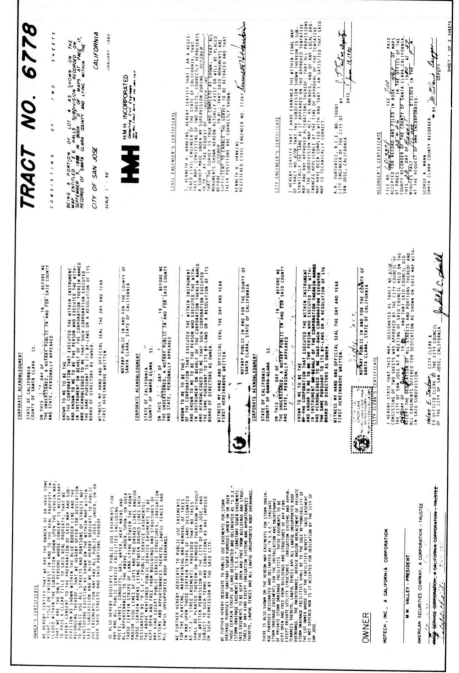

Fig. 2-15 (a) Sheet 1 of tract map; (b) sheet 2 of tract map. (*Courtesy of H.M.H., Incorporated, San Jose, CA.*)

32

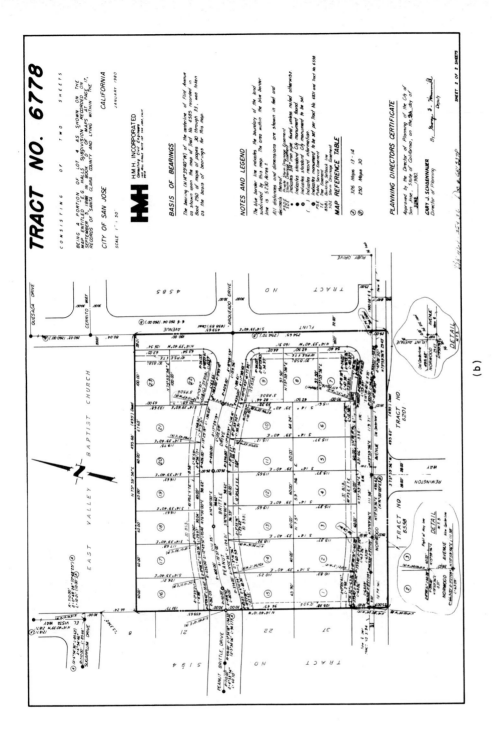

33

The format for including the material on the various types of plans will vary between areas, engineering firms, clients, times, and jobs. All the necessary information for a simple job might be included on a single sheet with a title such as "Grading and Drainage Plan." A large complicated job may have several sets of plans each containing 50 or more sheets. The number of sheets is determined by how many are needed to clearly show what is proposed and limited only by how many sheets make a set unwieldy.

Master Plans

Agencies that are responsible for providing and/or regulating facilities for the public, view the storm drainage, sanitary sewerage, water supply, or traffic plans differently than an engineer involved in a single project. One project is just one piece of a giant puzzle. That piece must be made to fit the whole puzzle—the master plan. The master plan of each affected agency must be consulted before work on the site plans begins.

Demolition Plans

When construction begins, demolition plans will be the first to be used. The purpose of demolition plans is to show what is to be saved and what is to be demolished so contractors can clear the way for the new construction. The plan is made on a reproducible copy of the topography map.

Special care should be taken to verify that all underground utilities or other facilities have been shown. It is not unusual for a job to be shut down because an abandoned irrigation conduit that is not shown on the plans is uncovered. Work cannot continue until it is determined what the conduit carries. There can be serious consequences of ripping up a 4-in high-pressure gas line or even a water main. When the presence of a large, high-pressure gas main is known, it must be marked with an obnoxious note such as the word **DANGER** spelled out in bold letters followed by a boldly printed note of what the danger is.

The limits of demolition should be clear and equipment kept back a safe distance from fences and walls owned by neighbors, If excavation is required, a soils engineer should be consulted about what precautions must be taken to protect adjacent structures.

Where a portion of sidewalk or other concrete area is to be preserved, there should be a note to "saw-cut or break at a joint" to ensure a professional, finished product. When some, but not all, trees or other amenities are to be saved, they must be marked in the field with an unmistakable message such as a fence erected clearly for the purpose of protecting that object. When the site is stripped of obstacles and the rubble has been cleared away, the site is ready for grading.

Grading Plans

Before concrete and pipes can be laid and building foundations begun, the site must be compacted to provide a solid, stable base. The surrounding area must be sculptured to slope away from the buildings to provide drainage, and the parking lots and streets must be shaped and sloped to direct overland flow toward drainage facilities.

The grading plan shows elevations at appropriate locations. With these, the survey crew marks the horizontal locations with wooden stakes and 2-in × 2-in wooden hubs. The stake identifies the elevation and the amount of cut or fill required above or below the top of the hub.

Construction Plans

When the grading is done, the work on the structures can begin. The construction plans show the horizontal and vertical locations of the structures as well as cross sections and whatever other details and instructions may be necessary to build the streets, drainage facilities, sewers, water supply lines, and other utilities. A complete description of what is included on the construction plans is included below under "Elements of the Plans."

As-Built Plans

During the construction of a project, it may be necessary to make changes. If there was an error in the design or some unforeseen obstacle prevents construction of the facilities as designed, a problem will exist that must be solved in the field. Any field changes should be shown on construction plans. When the construction is complete and all changes are marked on the construction plans and dated, that set of plans becomes known as as-built plans.

Traffic Plans

Traffic plans illustrate the signing, striping, and signalization of streets and roads for a project. When they are drawn for renovation of existing streets or roads, they may be drawn in ink on mylars of aerial photographs. When the plans are for new streets, they may be drawn on copies of base maps[5] for construction plans.

Traffic plans may or may not be included in the plan set depending on the complexity of the project and the requirements of the agency having responsibilities for traffic control and safety. The plans can include traffic flow diagrams and signalization plans as well as the locations, sizes, and types of striping and other pavement markings. A civil engineer specializing in traffic engineering should be responsible for the preparation of traffic engineering plans.

Landscaping Plans

Large or complicated projects may require separate landscaping plans. Ordinarily the landscaping is designed by a landscape architect. The plans show the

---

[5]The term *base map* is a misnomer. It is really a plan drawing which shows little other than the lines delineating property and streets. The plan is copied and used for different types of plans of the same area. The specialized information is then added to the different copies.

location and types of the trees and plants to be used and various other information to ensure the success of the planting. A plan for irrigation is usually included.

Development Plans

Some builders of single-family, detached homes use a drawing of the lots with a variety of information to assist in the construction of the homes. This drawing may be called a "development plan" (not to be confused with a planned development described in the section on zoning). The plan is a drawing to scale of the subdivision's lot lines and streets. A footprint (outline of the house) is drawn on each lot. Other information that may be shown on each lot is the model number of the house, elevation type, colors, roofing, and/or siding type to be used. The building setback distances may be shown for laying out the foundation or for acquiring building permits. A finished grading plan may be shown. Any other information that will expedite the completion of the project can be included.

Elements of the Plans

The plans for a small, uncomplicated project can be complete on one sheet, but in most cases a set of plans is necessary. A very large or complicated project may require several sets of plans and specifications. The types of drawings usually included in a set of plans will be described in this section.

Cover Sheet (Title Page)

A set of plans with more than one sheet should include a cover sheet (Fig. 10-1). What should be included on the cover sheet varies from job to job. Some of the things that may be included are:

A vicinity or location map
A legend
The basis of bearings
A bench mark
General plan showing the entire project
A table of contents
An index of sheets
Cross sections
Details
General notes

The choice of what is to be shown should be determined by what the jurisdiction requires and what will facilitate use of the plans.

Plan Views

The interior sheets of a set of plans are the plan and profile sheets (Fig. 10-2). These sheets most often are divided lengthwise. The top half of the sheet is for the drawings of the plan view of the streets. The bottom half has a grid for drawing the profile view of the streets and underground utilities. This may be reversed with the profile on top and plan view on the bottom.

The plan view shows significant information such as the centerline, face of curb line, and property line as viewed from above (Fig. 2-16). It should also include all of the utilities and significant topography. Power poles, existing storm water inlets, existing roads (curbs or edges of pavement), trees, and other objects that might affect the design should be shown.

Profiles

The view from the side showing the slopes, vertical curves, and appurtenant structures of any linear aspect of a project is called a *profile*. When the profile is of a street, the profile line can be located at any convenient reference point

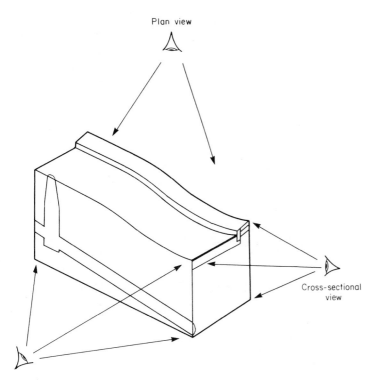

Fig. 2-16 Plan, profile, and cross-sectional views.

on the cross section (usually the centerline). Typically, the utility line profiles are included. Though there is some horizontal distance between the various profiles, they are projected onto the same vertical plane.

Cross Sections

Cross-sectional views show what is seen when an object is cut across with a vertical plane. Cross sections are used extensively in all areas of engineering and architecture. There are several examples of cross sections throughout this book.

When earthwork is to be calculated, cross-sectional views are necessary if the end area formula is to be used (Chapter 5). Cross sections are necessary on grading plans to portray how the finished product will look. They are also helpful when catch points at tops and toes of slopes are needed and the natural ground is sloped (Fig. 5-9).

Geometric cross sections (Fig. 6-17) show only dimensions and slopes; structural cross sections (Fig. 6-18) show types and depths of material to be used. When structural sections are shown, feet and hundredths of a foot may be used for some aspects of the drawing, and feet and inches may be used for another aspect of the same drawing. When making drawings that will include both types of information, it is helpful to use both an engineer's scale and an architect's scale (Table 2-1). If the scale of the drawing is 1 in = 4 ft and hundreths of a foot are used, the engineer's 40 scale is best because it divides each quarter inch (1 ft) into 10 increments. If the scale is 1 in = 4 ft and inches are used, the architect's scale is best because it divides each quarter inch into 12 increments.

TABLE 2-1

Architect's Scale	Engineer's Scale
1	10
½	20
¼	40

Details

Most sets of plans have some detail drawings. These include any structures that vary from the "Standard Plans" of typical structures approved for use within the jurisdiction. Detail drawings also show situations too small to be clear at the scale used for the surrounding area. The details may be shown on the cover sheet, on the sheet where the object is located, or on a special detail sheet depending on the number of details used and what will be most clear. The detail can be a plan, profile, or cross-sectional view, or any other type of drawing to assist in making the intent clear.

REFERENCES

Bourchard, Harry, and Moffitt, Francis H.: *Surveying,* International Textbook Company, Scranton, PA, 1965.

Brown, Curtis Maitland, and Eldridge, Winifield H.: *Evidence and Procedures for Boundary Location,* John Wiley & Sons, New York, 1962.

California Council of Civil Engineers & Land Surveyors: *Subdivision Map Act,* Sacramento, CA, 1983.

Davis, Raymond E., Foote, Francis S., and Kelly, Joe W.: *Surveying Theory and Practice,* McGraw-Hill Book Co., New York, 1966.

U.S. Department of the Interior: *Manual of Instructions for the Survey of the Public Lands of the United States,* 1973.

Wattles, William C.: *Land Survey Descriptions,* 10th ed., Gurdon H. Wattles, Orange, CA, 1974.

Chapter Three

Site Analysis

Site analysis should be done by experienced engineers with a firm grasp of the technology described in other chapters of this book. This subject is included here only as a natural beginning in the progression of a project. This chapter will be better understood and more useful after the novice has read the rest of this book.

Before engineering design is begun, a thorough analysis of the site must be made. This analysis should consist of an engineering feasibility investigation, a preliminary design, and a cost estimate. Ideally, this analysis is done at the time the client is considering several sites. This way, an intelligent choice among alternatives, based on comparisons of development and operating costs, can be made. Only the engineering feasibility will be discussed here. The preliminary design and cost estimate will be included in Chap. 4.

A Site Analysis Checklist is included (Fig. 3-1). Use it to collect information. Opposite Responsible Jurisdiction in the space provided for remarks, put such information as "Main Street will have to be improved to 106-ft width according to George Smith of Springfield," or "Solar access for south side of Main Street is required." Any of the items on the checklist that are not compatible with the proposed development may stop the project. Find out before thousands of dollars have been spent for planning, design, and fees.

Keep in mind budget constraints for the analysis. Preparing a formal report is foolish if the client has budgeted only enough for a few, quick phone calls. This chapter describes the procedure to use for a complete, formal report. A judgment should be made as to how much material can be included in the report.

SITE ANALYSIS CHECKLIST

Date assignment received: Date finished report required:

Assessor's map number _____   Size _____

Owner: Developer:

Description of location:

Description of environment:

Description of site:

Existing zoning _____   Required zoning _____

	YES	NO
Planning Commission hearing	_____	_____
City Council meeting	_____	_____
Annexation	_____	_____
Parcel map	_____	_____
Other:	_____	_____

Responsible Jurisdiction   **Remarks**

Streets:

Sanitary district:

Flood control district:

Water supply district:

Electricity:

Gas:

Telephone:

Cable TV:

Other:

Reports and Permits Required

	YES	NO
E.I.R.	_____	_____
Traffic	_____	_____
Air pollution	_____	_____
Noise pollution	_____	_____
Water	_____	_____
Geological	_____	_____
Soils	_____	_____
Archaeology	_____	_____
Historical	_____	_____
School impacts	_____	_____
Flood control district	_____	_____
Highway encroachment	_____	_____
Bays and harbors	_____	_____
Fish and game	_____	_____
Solar access	_____	_____

Figure 3-1. Site analysis checklist.

41

ZONING CONSIDERATIONS

Although zoning considerations are within the domain of planning, rather than engineering, it is important to be acquainted with them. Find out how the property is zoned. If the zoning is not appropriate, find out what steps to pursue to get the zoning changed and how long they will take. Typically, zoning changes require public hearings, and hearing dates may not be available for 6 months or even a year. Find out what the appeal procedures and time frames are in case the proposed change fails.

Zoning affects all sites, but each site is unique in the particular patchwork of jurisdictions that can impose constraints on development. Since the Environmental Protection Act was passed, an environmental impact report has been required on most development projects. If the site is small, it may be exempt from the report. But, the exemption must be established formally through specific procedures. Some other areas of concern that may require reports, clearances, and/or special permits are: flood control, traffic, school district impacts, archaeological resources, historic sites, noise and air pollution, scenic impacts, solar access, landslide hazards, and earthquake faults. These are examples of just a few of the things that can impact development costs. Be alert to them.

GETTING EXISTING PLANS

The next step is to get the plans for the existing streets and utilities. Plans are usually available from the public works or engineering departments of the city or county where the property is located. The water, gas, and electrical lines may be within the jurisdiction of the city.

Storm and Sanitary

If the site is in a city and the sewer plans are not available there or from a special district, the sewers may have been installed before the site was annexed to the city. Then, the plans may be at county offices. In developed areas, look at plans for the improvement of adjacent tracts. Plans of adjacent tracts will show not only the sewers installed with those sites, but the previously existing facilities they are connected to. In some cases, utilities are located in easements on private property rather than within public rights-of-way. The designs for the construction of the storm and sanitary sewers are usually on the same plans, if not as construction drawings, then as existing or proposed lines. Get copies of plans showing all adjacent utilities. The plans collected now will be used by the project engineer to indicate inverts and to help determine horizontal locations of existing lines. Elevations from different sets of plans may be taken from different bench marks, so it is not the elevation of inverts that is important, but rather the depth of the manhole, i.e., the difference between the manhole rim and the invert.

In many areas, the storm and sanitary sewerage systems are the responsibility of special districts. The boundaries of these districts seldom coincide with the city limits' lines. Whoever is responsible for each system will have a master sewer plan. The master plan will show the entire network of sewers within that district as well as proposed sewer lines. The agent will know which sewers are available.

In some areas, the sewage treatment plant has reached capacity. That is, as much wastewater as can be processed is already reaching the plant or has been allocated so that no more connections to the system can be made. If this is the case, ask if plant expansion is planned and, if so, when capacity will be available. If no expansion is planned, ask if there is another sanitation district in the area that might be used or if the sewage can be treated with septic tanks. Do not give up easily. Remember, if a way to provide a sanitation system is not found, the site cannot be developed.

Streets and Signalization

Engineers in the city or county offices will dictate street dimensions and depths of sections as well as any necessary signalization. Plans of existing streets in the area, however, suggest what to use for the report and cost estimate. Signalization is an expensive item. If installation of signals might be required, check with the responsible department.

Other Utilities and Services

Ordinarily, storm and sanitary sewers are designed for gravity flow, so their depth and slope are critical factors. Other utilities can be designed around the sewer systems. For this reason, the exact location of the other utilities is of minor concern at this point. The major concern is if the site can be served. Remember to check on water, gas, electricity, garbage collection, telephones, and cable television. If services will have to be extended to the site, what will the costs be? Also, check to see if there will be a requirement to put aerial electrical and telephone lines underground. Usually, the information needed can be learned by calling utility companies. Ask their representative to send a copy of their facilities in the area of the site. Though these copies usually have a disclaimer, they will provide information for the project engineer and evidence of your sources in case a problem with the location of the utility comes up later. Some utility companies will not send copies, but will allow the information to be copied in their office. If time allows, make these copies to include in the file for the job. If the representative promises to send a copy, in a week or two, check if it has arrived; if not, call the representative and ask if it has been sent.

THE SITE

A visit to the site is imperative. The visit should be discussed with the client. If the purchase price is still being negotiated or the project is unpopular, the investigation should be made inconspicuously—possibly without entering the property. On the other hand, if the client owns the property and it is occupied, a call ahead can clear the way.

Taking Notes and Photographs

Plan to take careful notes on the site. Neat, orderly notes are worth the extra effort; they are more credible and are easier to use. Take along the following items:

1. Clip board and note pad.
2. Two small (100 to 500 scale) site maps. A copy of the assessor's map of the parcel should be available from the county assessor's office. Use one copy for marking utilities from existing plans, topography, and notes. Use the second copy to identify snapshots as described below.
3. Site Analysis Check List. Write comments in Remarks sections.
4. Different colored pencils.
5. 6-in scale.
6. 50- or 100-ft tape.
7. Camera. Use a Polaroid type to be sure that the snapshot does, in fact, show what is intended.
8. Extra film. A jammed film packet can cost valuable time and/or the opportunity to get pictures that are particularly needed.
9. Business cards or other identification.

Once pictures have been taken, identify what they show. Mark each snapshot with a number. Show that number on the copy of the assessor's map, at the location where the picture was taken, and use an arrow to show the direction the camera was pointed (Fig. 3-2). On a separate sheet, list the photos with a brief description of what is shown, e.g., (a) existing storm sewer outfall, (b) condition of existing pavement, (c) oak tree (Fig. 3-3). These pictures will be invaluable throughout the planning and design phases of the job.

Recognizing Significant Features

With experience, the significant features of any site will seem conspicuous. Look for manholes, water valves, gas valves, power and telephone lines, and storm water inlets. Verify the locations of the utilities previously copied from existing plans, or sketch utilities as they exist on one of the assessor's maps. Use different colored pencils for the utilities that can be identified, e.g., red for sanitary manholes, green for storm manholes, blue for water valves. A legend on the sketch will save repetitious notes (Fig. 3-4).

Do not assume that because there is evidence of a utility it is available. A sewer may be too shallow or already at capacity. Similar problems exist with other utilities as well. Walk around the boundary of the site. Look for other utility lines for which you may not have found plans. Look for alternate ways to service the site in case the obvious solution cannot be used. The importance of alternatives will be discussed further in other chapters of this book.

Notice the slope of the site. How much grading will have to be done? Are there rock outcroppings (Fig. 3-5)? Is the soil sandy, spongy, soggy? A soils engineer or geologist should be commissioned to prepare a preliminary report.

Is the site higher in elevation than the surrounding area? If it is, find out from the water supply agency if water is available at the elevation or whether a pump and/or storage tank will be required. If the site is lower than the surrounding area, storm water may pond there, the water table may be near the surface, or the existing sewer lines may be too shallow to be useful.

How much area will be draining across the site? The storm water entering

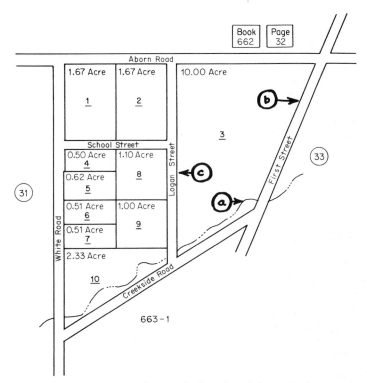

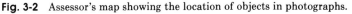

Fig. 3-2 Assessor's map showing the location of objects in photographs.

the site will have to be intercepted and prevented from flowing overland across the site. If the drainage basin upstream of the site is large, the drainage facilities will have to be large enough to accommodate the extra runoff.

Is there a river or stream running through the site? If so, look for high water marks on buildings and trees that will indicate if there has been flooding. Look at recent improvements adjacent to the waterway. There may be restrictions as to the finished floor elevation, or a flood plain corridor may have to be provided that will limit the buildable area. Open-space corridors in adjacent developments may indicate easements, flood plains, or fault zones.

Notice trees. They are a valuable amenity, and some jurisdictions limit which trees can and cannot be cut down. Note the type and condition of buildings on the site. What appears to be a worthless shack, in fact, may house the only

(a)

(b)

(c)

Fig. 3-3 Photographs taken at the site. (a) Existing storm sewer outfall; (b) condition of street; (c) oak tree.

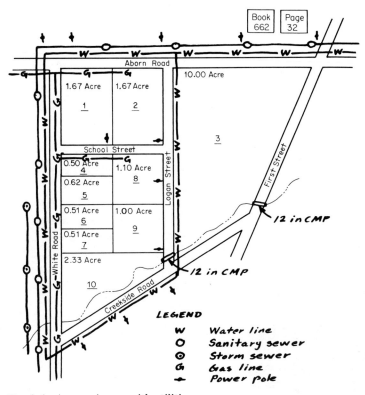

Fig. 3-4 Assessor's map with utilities.

Fig. 3-5 Rock outcroppings.

producing well for miles. Check it out. A stand pipe (Fig. 3-6) might be part of a defunct irrigation system or a blowoff valve for the town's main water supply line. There is no way that all the possibilities can be listed. Be alert to potential trouble. Before leaving the site, review the notes. Take one last look to see if anything was missed.

WRITING THE REPORT

When the investigation is complete, write the report. Start with an outline so the report will be clear and orderly. Have a table of contents so specific information can be found quickly. Include all pertinent information. (An example of a table of contents is included in Fig. 3-7.) Document resources. Give the names and titles of those who stated that signalization or a 24-in water main will be required, or that there will be partial reimbursement for oversized facilities.

By the time the body of the report is finished, it will be clear how the site differs from other sites. The extraordinary facilities and costs the site will

Fig. 3-6 Stand pipe.

require should now be known. Write a summary and put it at the front of the report. This way, the client will get the information needed easily. The information in the summary should *not* be a condensed version of the rest of the report, but rather a concise statement of selected information to describe what is unusual about the site. For instance, a part of the summary might read:

Though Clear Creek is 1500 ft to the south, and there is no evidence of flooding in or around the site, officials at Springfield Flood Control District state that it is within the flood plain of a 100-year storm and a flood plain zone will be required over the south 4 acres.
   If flood protection can be provided, development of the site should be nearly routine.

From this, the client can go directly to the section of the report dealing with flood protection for a broader explanation of what will be required and how

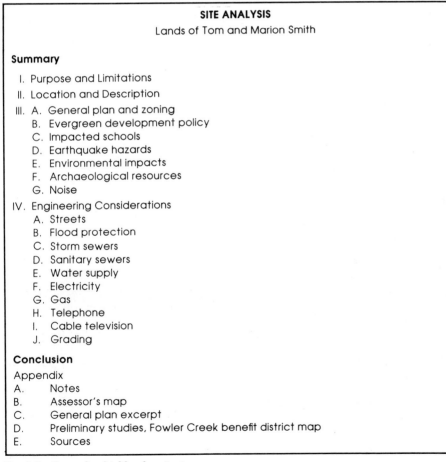

SITE ANALYSIS
Lands of Tom and Marion Smith

Summary

   I. Purpose and Limitations

  II. Location and Description

 III. A. General plan and zoning
      B. Evergreen development policy
      C. Impacted schools
      D. Earthquake hazards
      E. Environmental impacts
      F. Archaeological resources
      G. Noise

 IV. Engineering Considerations
      A. Streets
      B. Flood protection
      C. Storm sewers
      D. Sanitary sewers
      E. Water supply
      F. Electricity
      G. Gas
      H. Telephone
      I. Cable television
      J. Grading

Conclusion

Appendix
A.   Notes
B.   Assessor's map
C.   General plan excerpt
D.   Preliminary studies, Fowler Creek benefit district map
E.   Sources

Fig. 3-7 Example of table of contents.

much it will cost. If interested, the client will also be able to find out who the officials are who stated the requirements and what a "100-year storm" is.

REFERENCES

DeChiara, Joseph, and Koppelman, Lee E.: *Site Planning Standards*, McGraw-Hill Book Co., New York, 1978.

The National Association of Home Builders: *Land Development Manual,* Washington, DC, 1974.

The National Association of Home Builders: *Land Development 2,* Washington, DC, 1981.

Chapter Four

Preliminary Engineering

The first step of preliminary engineering is the site analysis. If a thorough site analysis report was made, much of the preliminary engineering is done. If not, the feasibility of the project should be investigated before more time and money are spent.

The primary purpose of preliminary engineering is an evaluation of the costs of construction. The expected cost of the project must be known before construction loans can be applied for and cash flow evaluated. Usually, people trained as planners will prepare the street and lot layouts for the subdivision map, but engineers should understand the criteria and be prepared if asked to design a subdivision. The preliminary engineering and cost estimate should be done by an experienced engineer.

PRELIMINARY DESIGN

The layout of the streets and lots for subdivisions are affected by several factors—the locations of existing streets and utilities, the slope of the land, the presence of legal limitations, natural amenities, traffic flows, and criteria relative to the lots.

The most economical use of a site will maximize the number of lots while minimizing the space occupied by streets. To accomplish this, several layouts should be designed. The minimum areas and frontages of lots may be dictated by zoning ordinances. Some developers have house plans designed with dimensions to fit frontage and side yard setback requirements exactly so there is not an inch of frontage extra. There is increasing use of town houses and patio

Driveway

Fig. 4-1 Driveway following the contours of the hill.

homes[1] to make the greatest use of street frontages and reduce the relative cost of street and utility construction. Where there are existing or proposed easements, the lots and streets should be designed so that easements fall within the street or at the edges of lots so as not to encumber full use of the lots.

It is undersirable to use long, straight streets. Such streets encourage speeders and are boring. However, the cost of engineering, staking, and construction of curves is greater than straight lines, so curves should be used judiciously. On hillside sites, the desirability or necessity of curvilinear streets is clear. Street grades must be within an acceptable range for safety. Routes that curve around a hill rather than go directly to the top are not as steep. Also a street that follows the contours of the hill (Fig. 4-1), rather than going directly up the side (Fig. 4-2), will be less noticeable to those observing the hillside from below.

When laying out the lots on hillside sites, allowance in the sizes of the lots must be made for slopes. This allowance cannot be estimated. Slope requirements and building setbacks must be determined. The cost of grading is a major expense. As much as possible, the natural contour of the land should be used. The use of split-level house plans should be encouraged. Lot drainage will have to be considered. The appearance of the homes from the street level should please the eye. Cut or fill slopes of more than 8 ft should be avoided if visible from the street.

---

[1]A patio home is built with one windowless exterior wall which is placed on a side property line. The total required distance between buildings is then put on the other side, creating a side yard wide enough to be useful for outdoor living. This makes more efficient use of the lot.

PRELIMINARY ENGINEERING

When a preliminary design is selected, the preliminary engineering can begin. Occasionally, the preliminary engineering and estimates are not requested until tentative map approval is completed. When a tentative map is available with its conditions of approval, it should be used for preliminary engineering and cost estimates.

The object of preliminary engineering is to do an initial layout of sewers and other utilities so that a cost estimate can be made. Do not let the preliminary nature of the task cause you to be careless in your analysis. The preliminary work may be accepted and refinement of calculations made without further analysis. Make the preliminary engineering layout on a print of the preliminary or tentative map. List quantities and unit costs used on the map so you will have a record (Fig. 4-3).

Maps

When a preliminary layout is selected, the tentative map can be prepared and approvals procedures begun. Any necessary transfer of land can be begun as

Fig. 4-2 Street going directly up the side of a hill.

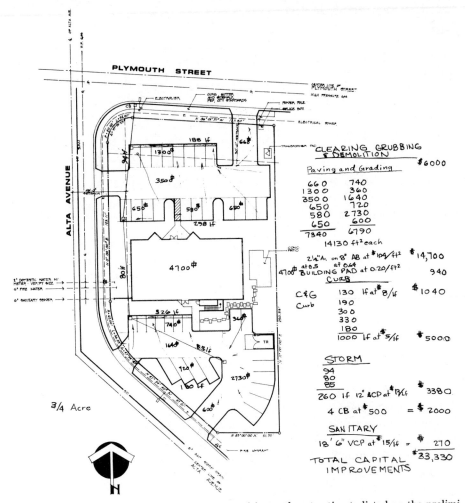

Fig. 4-3 Preliminary engineering design, quantities, and cost estimate listed on the preliminary plan.

well. Where it will be necessary to install utility lines or ditches through private property, easements or rights-of-way must be purchased. To accomplish this, title reports should be ordered, legal descriptions prepared, and negotiations begun. This process should be started as soon as the need for the easement is realized. The smaller the investment made before all required property is secure, the less the risk involved and the better the client's bargaining position.

When the tentative map is approved, there will be conditions of approval to be satisfied. The surveying calculations and drafting of the subdivision or parcel maps should be started. This procedure, as well as any legal descriptions, takes time and expertise, so there are costs associated with it. An estimate of how much it will cost should be made.

Streets

The preliminary map will provide the layout of the streets. The standards of the jurisdiction for the geometric requirements indicate the street widths and curb, gutter, and sidewalk requirements. The standards are based on the amount of traffic expected. The structural section is based on traffic expected and soil conditions. The requirements of the structural section will not be known in the early stages, but the preliminary estimate can be based on other streets of similar use (width) in the area. This information can be taken from adjacent subdivisions. Be aware, however, that the structural section may not be indicative if the adjacent streets were built much earlier.

There are often two or more types of streets within one project. A *cul-de-sac* may have a shallower section than a primary street. Because of this, each type of street will have to be estimated separately. The streets can be shown as so many square feet of pavings, e.g., 5½ in of AC (asphaltic concrete) on 10 in of AB (aggregate base), or 4 in AC on 6 in of AB. On some projects the asphalt and aggregate may be shown in tons rather than square footage.

Storm Sewers

A rough estimate of the expected rainfall runoff must be made. The master plan of the storm drainage agency must be consulted. If the site is surrounded by previously developed sites, the runoff may be the result of only what falls on the site. Otherwise, an estimate of runoff from adjacent areas must be made. Determining the runoff area is described in Chap. 8, Storm Drainage, under the heading Hydrology. If an area master plan is not available, a USGS map can be used to delineate drainage basins.

The site and those adjacent areas which will contribute to storm runoff through the site should be divided into drainage basins so that an estimate of the number and location of storm water inlets can be made. The locations of manholes can be laid out. The sizes of pipes can be estimated based on the runoff and approximate slope of the ground.

Sanitary Sewers

The initial layout of the sanitary sewers is simpler than that of storm sewers since every building must be served. If the mains will serve only the buildings on the project and it is a residential site, the minimum size conduit may be adequate throughout. The responsible agency dictates the flows to use for each household, a peak flow factor, and infiltration rate. Manholes and flushing inlets should be included in the layout and cost estimate.

Grading

Clearing, grubbing, and demolition are items usually included under grading. These items are the least tangible items to estimate. Certainly, if the site is covered with orchard, clearing and grubbing will cost more than if the site is an open field. If there is paving to be removed from the site, demolition should be estimated on the basis of square footage. It may be appropriate to estimate clearing based on acreage. Demolition of buildings should be estimated on the number and sturdiness of the buildings to be demolished. A contractor expecting to be given the demolition contract may be willing to provide an estimate.

Previously unimproved sites require removal of organic material from the soil. The depth will vary from site to site. The soils report should address this and recommend the depth of soil to be removed, but at this early stage the soils report is not likely to be available. The depth used for other sites in the area can be used. Otherwise, the estimate is little more than a guess. Fortunately the cost of clearing, grubbing, and demolition is usually a small portion of the cost of construction.

Grading can be one of the most important aspects of a cost estimate. This is particularly true if the site will have to be built up and if earth must be brought in from miles away. Though it is unusual, it is possible that a contractor will pay to be allowed to dump excess material from another site. Most often if material is needed, it is expensive to locate and transport to the site. In a metropolitan area, the cost of imported material can make a project infeasible.

In most cases, the earthwork can be made to balance. The cost of grading for the streets and pads is based on removing the plant material and compacting the soil to the specifications of the soils engineer. The cost of grading the pads will be charged at a different rate than streets and parking lots, so it should be listed separately on the cost estimate.

Water Lines

If the water supply company will be installing the water systems, the cost of providing water services should be based on their estimate. If the responsibility for the design of the water supply is with the engineering consultant, an estimate must be made. A layout of the lines, remembering loops, should be made.

Some water companies have significant charges if a line is to have a wet tap. Mains, laterals, water meters, fire hydrants, air-relief and blow-off valves must be included in the estimate.

Lighting

The cost of installing electroliers should be included. An estimate of the number needed should be based on the type of lamp and spacing required by the jurisdiction.

COST ESTIMATING

When the initial layout of the streets and utilities is complete, the preliminary estimate can be prepared. List the quantities on the same print used for the preliminary layout of utilities (Fig. 4-3). This way, if the final cost of construction is different from the preliminary estimate, a comparison of designs can be made and the reason for the difference determined.

Most engineering firms have a list of items that might be necessary to include (Fig. 4-4). By using the list, items are less likely to be missed. Of course, there may be items to include which are not on the standard form.

Count the various items needed, measure the lengths of conduits, and calculate the square footage of paving and other quantities. Make no attempt to be precise. If a length of pipe is between 180 and 190 ft, use 190. If there is a minimal amount of grading of the site needed and the quantity is to be in cubic yards, assume earthwork as 2 ft over the site. Be conservative. Clients get loans based on your estimates; if they are too low, the client may be in financial trouble. On the other hand, if your estimate is high and you cannot justify it, clients will take their business elsewhere. Compare the estimate with similar projects. If the costs vary significantly, be sure the differences can be justified.

When the initial layout of the streets and utilities is complete and the quantities estimated, the preliminary estimate can be prepared. The map used for the estimate should be identified at the top, e.g., "Engineers Preliminary Cost Estimate for Carlsen Property, based on a 100 scale preliminary site plan dated June 8, 1983." This way, if the final plan is significantly different and the costs differ from the estimate, the reason for the difference can be understood. The format used will vary between engineers, clients, jobs, and times. Each estimate should be tailored to the job.

There may be reasons to segregate the project into parts for the estimate. If the project is large, it may be constructed in phases. It may be desirable to separate the on-site and off-site work. Various conditions, such as an adjacent property being developed, may change with time; so required work and cost will vary from time to time. This should be explained in the notes section and comparison of costs with time listed.

Factors Affecting Costs

A unit cost will be allocated to each item on the cost estimate listing. These unit costs will vary from job to job. Costs are affected by:

Date: _____

Job No.: _____

ENGINEER'S PRELIMINARY COST ESTIMATE

Quantity	Units	Description of Item	Unit Price	Total
		Planning		
		Annexation		$ _____
		Zone change		$ _____
		Preliminary planning		$ _____
		Preparation of tentative subdivision map		$ _____
		Preparation of final map		$ _____
		Preparation of land descriptions for easements		$ _____
		Subtotal		$ _____
		Surveying		
		Boundary survey		$ _____
		Topographic survey		$ _____
		Reference for aerial survey		$ _____
		Aerial topography		$ _____
		Subtotal		$ _____
		Paving and Grading		
_____	L.S.	Demolition	$ _____	$ _____
_____	acre	Clearing and grubbing	$ _____	$ _____
_____	ft^2	Street grading	$ _____	$ _____
_____	ft^2	Lot grading	$ _____	$ _____
_____	ft^2	_____ in AC/_____ in AB/_____ in ASB	$ _____	$ _____
_____	ft^2	_____ in AC/_____ in AB/_____ in ASB	$ _____	$ _____
_____	ft^2	_____ in AC/_____ in AB/_____ in ASB	$ _____	$ _____
_____	lf	Curb and gutter (includes cushion)	$ _____	$ _____
_____	lf	Vertical curb (includes cushions)	$ _____	$ _____
_____	lf	Stick-on curb	$ _____	$ _____
_____	lf	AC berm	$ _____	$ _____
_____	ft^2	Sidewalk	$ _____	$ _____
_____	each	Driveway approach	$ _____	$ _____
_____	each	Handicap ramp	$ _____	$ _____
_____	ft^2	Valley gutter	$ _____	$ _____
_____	each	Barricades	$ _____	$ _____
_____	each	Monuments	$ _____	$ _____
_____	each	Street signs	$ _____	$ _____
		Subtotal		$ _____
		Storm Sewers		
_____	each	Storm water inlet	$ _____	$ _____
_____	each	Catch basins	$ _____	$ _____
_____	each	Standard manhole	$ _____	$ _____
_____	each	Special manhole	$ _____	$ _____
_____	each	Outfall structure	$ _____	$ _____
_____	lf	Concrete lined ditch	$ _____	$ _____
_____	lf	Gunite ditch	$ _____	$ _____
_____	lf	Unlined ditch	$ _____	$ _____
_____	lf	12-in RCP	$ _____	$ _____
_____	lf	15-in RCP	$ _____	$ _____
_____	lf	18-in RCP	$ _____	$ _____
_____	lf	12-in PVC	$ _____	$ _____
_____	lf	15-in PVC	$ _____	$ _____

| | | | Date: _____ |
| | | | Job No.: _____ |

Quantity	Units	Description of Item	Unit Price	Total
_____	lf	18-in PVC	$ _____	$ _____
_____	lf	6-in PMP	$ _____	$ _____
_____	lf	8-in PMP	$ _____	$ _____
_____	lf	12-in CSP	$ _____	$ _____
_____	lf	15-in CSP	$ _____	$ _____
_____	lf	12-in ACP	$ _____	$ _____
_____	lf	15-in ACP	$ _____	$ _____
_____	lf	18-in ACP	$ _____	$ _____
		Subtotal		$ _____

Sanitary Sewers

Quantity	Units	Description of Item	Unit Price	Total
_____	each	4-in laterals	$ _____	$ _____
_____	each	8-in laterals	$ _____	$ _____
_____	lf	6-in VCP	$ _____	$ _____
_____	lf	8-in VCP	$ _____	$ _____
_____	lf	10-in VCP	$ _____	$ _____
_____	each	Standard manhole	$ _____	$ _____
_____	each	Manhole w/outside drop	$ _____	$ _____
_____	each	Flushing inlet	$ _____	$ _____
		Subtotal		$ _____

Water

Quantity	Units	Description of Item	Unit Price	Total
_____	lf	8-in concrete pipe	$ _____	$ _____
_____	lf	10-in concrete pipe	$ _____	$ _____
_____	lf	12-in RCP	$ _____	$ _____
_____	each	Air-relief valves	$ _____	$ _____
_____	each	Blow-off valves	$ _____	$ _____
_____	each	1-in lateral	$ _____	$ _____
_____	each	1½-in lateral	$ _____	$ _____
_____	each	2-in lateral	$ _____	$ _____
_____	each	Water services including meter and meter box	$ _____	$ _____
_____	each	Wet tap	$ _____	$ _____
		Subtotal		$ _____

Miscellaneous

Quantity	Units	Description of Item	Unit Price	Total
		Storm sewer fee		$ _____
		Sanitary sewer fee		$ _____
		Water system fee		$ _____
		Fire hydrant fee		$ _____
		Signing and striping		$ _____
		Underground electrical lines _____ FF @ $ _____/FF		$ _____
		Bond premiums _____% of $ _____		$ _____
		City engineer inspection and permit		$ _____
		Civil engineering		$ _____
		Contingencies		$ _____
		Subtotal		$ _____

Fig. 4-4 Checklist of items for estimate.

ENGINEER'S PRELIMINARY COST ESTIMATE
for
TRACT 7000

Based on a 60 scale Preliminary Site Plan
prepared by Carter Engineers, Inc. dated January 20, 1981

Quantity	Units	Description of Item	Unit Price	Total
		On Site		
		Grading and Paving		
	L.S.	Demolition clearing and grubbing	$ 500.00	$ 500.
42,359	ft^2	Street grading	0.30	12,710.
39,353	ft^2	2-in AC/6-in AB	0.90	35,420.
291	lf	Type "A" curb and gutter (incl. cushion)	5.00	1,460.
1,713	lf	Type "B" vertical curb	4.00	6,850.
3,480	ft^2	Sidewalk (incl. cushion)	1.20	4,180.
3	each	Lot grading	400.00	1,200.
1631	ft^2	Valley gutter	3.00	4,890.
		Total on-site grading and paving cost		$ 67,210.
		Storm Sewers		
2	each	Catch basins	450.00	$ 900.
3	each	Standard manholes	800.00	2,400.
223	lf	12-in RCP	12.00	2,680.
		Total on-site storm sewer cost		$ 5,980.
		Sanitary Sewers		
420	lf	4-in sanitary lateral	5.00	$ 2,100.
727	lf	6-in VCP main	7.15	5,200.
5	each	Standard manholes	800.00	4,000.
1	each	Flushing inlets	80.00	80.
		Total on-site sanitary sewer cost		$ 11,380.
		Off Site		
		Paving and Grading		
	L.S.	Demolition	$ 500.00	$ 500.
7,520	ft^2	Street grading	0.30	2,260.
5,600	ft^2	10-in AC/9-in AB	2.75	15,400.
2,880	ft^2	2½-in AC overlay	0.50	1,440.
160	lf	Curb and gutter (incl. cushion)	5.00	800.
599	ft^2	Sidewalk (incl. cushion)	1.20	720.
1	each	Driveway approaches	300.00	300.
1	each	Electroliers (incl. conduit and conductor)	1,400.00	1,400
94	lf	Barricades	10.00	940.
		Total off-site paving and grading cost		$ 23,760.

Fig. 4-5 Example of cost estimate.

Quantity	Units	Description of Item	Unit Price	Total
		Storm Sewers		
1	each	Catch basins	$ 450.00	$ 450.
3	each	Standard manholes	800.00	2,400.
346	lf	12-in RCP	12.00	4,150.
5	lf	24-in RCP	26.00	130.
		Total off-site storm sewers cost		$ 7,130.
		Sanitary Sewers		
285	lf	6-in VCP main	7.15	$ 2,040.
2	each	Standard manholes	800.00	1,600.
		Total off-site sanitary sewers cost		$ 3,640.
		Miscellaneous		
		Storm sewer fee		$ 4,430.
		Sanitary sewer fee		$ 10,660.
		Underground electrical lines 160 FF at $6.00/FF		960.
		Bond premium 1.5% of $34,530.		520.
		Contingencies at 10% of $119,100.		11,910.
		Total miscellaneous cost		$ 28,480.
		Summary		
		On site		$ 84,570.
		Off site		34,530.
		Miscellaneous		28,480.
			Total	$147,580.

Estimated cost per unit $\dfrac{\$147,580}{64 \text{ units}} = \$2300.$

NOTES:

1. This estimate is prepared as a guide only, is based upon incomplete information, and is subject to possible change. Carter Engineers, Inc., makes no warranty, either express or implied, that actual costs will not vary from the amounts indicated and assumes no liability for such variances.

2. The estimate does not include:
   a. Civil engineering costs
   b. Soils engineering report
   c. Fencing
   d. Building-related costs and fees
   e. Financing charges
   f. Landscaping and finish grading
   g. Reimbursable agreements or refundable deposits

3. Pavement thickness is estimated and will not be determined until after soils testing has been performed.

4. Water costs and miscellaneous fees are not included in this estimate.

5. Costs are based on estimated current prices without provision for inflation.

6. This estimate does not include costs of acquiring storm and sanitary easement through the Smith property.

1. The size of the job. The unit cost of material and installation for a large job is less than for a small job. The overhead costs and the cost of transporting equipment and material to a site will often be nearly the same for two units as for twenty-two units.
2. The location of the site. Again, transportation costs depend on distance and accessibility of the site. This is particularly true in the case of imported earth.
3. The client. Some public agencies are notorious for elaborate specifications and fastidious inspectors. Contractors know that these factors will be costly in time and money.
4. The engineer. If incomplete or incorrect plans have cost a contractor time and money on a job previously designed by a particular engineer, the contractor may be reluctant to work with that engineer again or may pad the costs with a large contingency factor.
5. The season. Longer days and dry weather allow work to be accomplished more quickly, thus more cheaply.
6. The economy. If the economy is booming and the contractors have all the work they can handle, the estimate may be high because there is not much incentive to do more work. If economic times are poor or a contractor is trying to establish a new business, the contractor may hold down the costs to get the job.
7. Financial factors. The cash flow is often an important factor. If payments are to be based on work completed, the unit costs of work done in the early stages of construction may be high, and those of work done in the late stages may be relatively low. This gives the contractor working capital at the beginning of the project.

Keep these influences in mind when selecting unit prices to use for the estimate. The values you select to use for unit prices when making estimates should be based on recent experience. Keep a copy of each estimate you make for reference. When a job has "gone to bid," get the prices the contractors used whenever possible. Some developers and public agencies use a *spread sheet* (Fig. 11-1) which lists the unit price estimated by contractors for each item to be used. Where quantities are similar, take unit prices from the spread sheet of another job. When the job includes an unusual structure, it may be necessary to ask a contractor involved in that type of work for an estimate. One other source to use in determining the value of contract items is one of the books published each year which lists unit prices of construction material.

Miscellaneous Costs and Fees

There are always some costs and fees that are not for material and installation and do not fit into the other listed categories. There are fees to be paid for connection to storm and sanitary sewers and water systems. There may be permits for encroachment into streams or highway rights-of-way. The cost of putting power and telephone lines underground may be listed here. Some areas may have fees to help offset increased costs of fire and police protection and for schools and parks.

There will be the cost of engineering both by the design consultant and the responsible jurisdiction. These fees are usually based on, or at least relative to, the cost of capital improvements.[2] There will be a completion bond to be paid. This too is relative to the cost of improvements. Contingencies is a category covering unforeseen expenses and is usually between 5 and 30 percent of the total cost of improvements.

Notes

The notes of the cost estimate are particularly important. Any assumptions used in making the estimate should be clearly explained. Where the responsibility for some costs are not clear, include this information in the notes. This way the developers can make a judgment whether or not to include those costs. State whether the costs used are at current value or include an inflation factor. Most engineers include a disclaimer that the estimate is only a guide, and they assume no responsibility for variances with actual costs. State possible costs that are not included such as sound walls, environmental impact reports, and soils reports.

Where the facilities required are oversized, the jurisdiction may give partial reimbursement to the developer for improvements larger than what is needed to serve the project. When this is the case, the anticipated reimbursement should be described. Refundable deposits, such as are sometimes required for water meters until the building is occupied, should be listed. Try to anticipate questions the developer may have, and provide the answers in the notes (Fig. 4-5).

[2]Capital improvements include all tangible items in place after construction. Fees are not included.

Chapter Five

Earthwork

Each site must be sculptured and compacted to provide suitable foundations for buildings and other structures and to direct storm water away from buildings. The activities necessary to accomplish this are called *earthwork*. Without proper preparation of the site, the finished product is subject to structural failures and inundation.

THE SOILS REPORT

An investigation of the soils and underlying geologic structures should be made for every site. A report of the investigation should be made by a qualified civil engineer and/or geologist specializing in soils science.

The soils engineer will visit the site, take soils samples, make borings at various locations, and, where earthquake faults are suspected, dig and study trenches. The cores resulting from the borings show the underlying strata. A three-dimensional view of the layers of earth and rock can be projected from the cores. Though the distribution of the soils is based on an educated guess, the unknowns are decreased and much useful information is provided. The presence of groundwater,[1] veins of hard rock, ancient or potential landslides, and the proximity of the site to earthquake faults is noted. A series of tests are performed on the soil to determine its strength, plasticity, potential for liquefaction, and permeability. This information will be useful to the architect and structural engineer in designing foundations, to the site engineer for designing

---

[1] The level of groundwater varies with the time of year and the character of the previous rainy season. If the seasons have not been typical or there is historical evidence that groundwater is a problem, further investigation is indicated.

paved surfaces and slopes, and to the contractor charged with grading the site. The site engineer should read the soils and geology reports in their entirety before beginning the grading plan.

The report should describe a maximum allowable slope. The allowable slope is based on the angle of repose for the soil. Using a steeper slope could result in slope failure (landslide). The slope will be described as the horizontal distance necessary for each foot of vertical height. For a slope of 2:1 there is 1 ft of vertical difference for every 2 ft of horizontal difference (Fig. 5-1). These slopes will be used for cut and fill areas between building pads, roadbeds, or other structures of different elevations, and between structures and natural ground. Where there will be very high cut or fill slopes (±20 ft), a bench is usually required in the slope. The bench will stop falling rocks and earth and will be used to catch and remove overland drainage.

The soil compressibility should be included in the report and is important to the site engineer. Typically, to provide an engineered base for structures, the soil must be 95 percent compacted. The natural earth in place normally is not compacted to 95 percent, and so, when compacted, more earth is required to occupy the same space. A clear demonstration of this can be seen when you fill a cup loosely with sand and clear off the excess sand level with the top of the cup. After you tap the cup several times, the sand will compact, and the cup

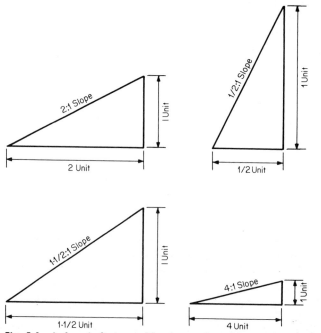

Fig. 5-1 A slope is designated by the number of feet (units) horizontal for each one foot (unit) of vertical difference.

will no longer be full. The same is true for earthwork. All sites require some excavation and filling. If the earthwork is measured in cubic yards for design and estimation purposes, more than a cubic yard of excavation will be required for each cubic yard to be filled. The percentage of difference (expressed as a portion of 1) is called the compaction or shrinkage factor.

It is desirable to have the earthwork on a site "balance." The earthwork on a site is said to balance when no import or export of material is required. To accomplish a balance, a volume of earth to allow for shrinkage must be included in the calculations. The relationship used to determine the amount of earth needed, compensating for shrinkage, is shown in Eq. 5-1.

$$V_R = \frac{V}{1.00 - S} \tag{5-1}$$

where V_R = volume of compacted earth (fill) required, cubic yards
$\quad\quad V$ = volume of uncompacted earth (excavation), cubic yards
$\quad\quad S$ = shrinkage factor

Example 5-1

Determine the volume of earth needed to accommodate the shrinkage factor. The shrinkage factor is 0.15. The volume of uncompacted earth is 4560 yd³.

Solution

Use Eq. 5-1 to determine the total volume of earth required.

$$\begin{aligned} V_R &= \frac{V}{1.00 - S} \\ &= \frac{4560 \text{ yd}^3}{1.00 - 0.15} \\ &= 5365 \text{ yd}^3 \end{aligned} \tag{5-1}$$

Calculate the difference between the volume of compacted earth and the volume of uncompacted earth.

$$5365 \text{ yd}^3 - 4560 \text{ yd}^3 = 805 \text{ yd}^3$$

The amount of fill to allow for the compaction factor is 805 yd³.

A bulking factor should be applied to volumes of earth where the in-place material is extremely dense, as with rock. The bulking factor represents the percentage that densely compacted earth will increase in volume when excavated.

The soils report should recommend types of building foundations suited to the soils and geologic conditions. Structural sections for streets and parking lots should also be recommended. The structural section will be based on the volume and weight characteristics of the traffic expected. This is called the *traffic index* (TI). There will be a range of possibilities. Thicker asphaltic concrete

(AC) requires less thickness of aggregate base (AB). Cement-treated base (CTB) may be used in place of, or in conjunction with, aggregate base. Where practical, list the alternatives on the plans or in the specifications. Where the native soils have poor structural qualities or are expansive, the soils report may recommend importation of soils better suited to providing a subbase for structures.

DESIGNING THE GRADING PLAN

The first step in the construction of a site is the rough grading. A grading plan must be designed for the location of building pads, streets, and other structures. Information must be put on the plan to direct survey crews in placing 2-in $\times$ 2-in wooden hubs (guineas) and stakes. The elevation of the top of the hub is determined by the survey crew. A survey stake is placed next to the hub. A brief description of what the hub marks and the amount to cut or fill from the top of the hub is written on the stake. ER TC, C 1.26 indicates that the hub is located at the end of the curb return (ER) and that the earth must be cut away 1.26 ft below the top of the hub to the top-of-curb (TC) elevation. A construction crew member called a *guineahopper* will read and call out to the equipment operator whether to cut away or fill in earth, and the depth to cut or fill.

Elevations

Of prime importance in understanding the various elements of the grading plans as well as the other aspects of design is the concept of elevations.

When the term *elevation* is used, it may refer to an actual elevation (vertical distance in feet above mean sea level), or it may refer to a vertical distance above an assumed elevation. Though the dimension of the elevation is in feet, it is customary to show elevations without designation. All maps and plans using elevations should have a *bench mark* (BM). The bench mark is a vertical reference point. The bench mark may be a brass disk set in concrete by the United States Geological Survey (USGS) or some other agency, and tied to mean sea level, but it can be anything that has a permanent elevation and can be referenced. A cross marked in a curb and referred to on plans with a particular elevation is often used. Some cities require that all plans be referenced to city standard bench marks.

On projects where there is no existing bench mark in the vicinity, a bench mark can be established with an assumed elevation. The elevation assumed should be high enough so no point related to the project will have a negative elevation. There are areas where the land is below sea level and will have negative elevations, but when an assumed elevation is to be used for the bench mark, negative elevations should be avoided.

Care should be taken when using elevations from existing plans. The bench marks used to design different projects are often taken from different sources; so to the relation between elevations on the projects will not be true. The elevation for a physical object taken from one bench mark will be different from an elevation for the same object taken from another bench mark, unless the two bench marks refer to a common bench mark. Even then, there may be some differences due to the degree of precision or errors. Where two or more sets of plans are to be tied together, a bench mark equation should be established and described on the plans. An example is:

Rim elevation for sanitary manhole on Main Street at Spring Street is 139.68 from Tract 5555 and is 140.03 from Tract 5560.

In this case, if the bench mark for Tract 5560 is to be used on the new project, but ties must be made to objects in Tract 5555, 0.35 ft (140.03-139.68) must be added to all elevations taken from Tract 5555.

Before design is begun on the grading plan, elevations should be shown wherever they must be considered in the design. This includes elevations for existing and proposed:

1. Tops of curbs at
   a. Property lines
   b. Beginning and ends of horizontal curves
   c. Beginnings, ends, and high or low points in vertical curves
   d. High and low points in street profiles
2. Ditch flow lines
3. Existing streets being met
4. The bases of trees and other amenities to remain

Contours

Lines connecting points of equal elevation are called *contours* (Fig. 5-2). They are usually plotted for even elevations of 1, 2, or 5 ft. Where the terrain is very flat, the 1-ft contour interval is used and intermediate elevations are spotted where the slope between contours is not uniform. In steep terrain, the contour interval may be 5 ft, 10 ft, or even greater. The steeper the slope, the closer the contours will be. Therefore, rather than fill the map with contour lines, a larger interval is used.

In surveying topography, the surveyor should have marked an elevation wherever there is a break in the slope. Therefore, it should be safe to assume that the ground between elevations slopes evenly. To locate the contour at elevation 196.0 between points with elevations of 196.8 and 195.4, divide the space into 14 equal spaces (196.8−195.4 = 1.4). Each space will equal 0.1 ft. Count up from the location of the 195.4 elevation six spaces, and you have the location of the 196.0 contour. It should be eight spaces down from the location of the 196.8 elevation. When several spots have been located for the 196.0 elevation, connect the spots creating the 196.0 contour.

When plotting or interpreting contours, remember:

1. Contour lines will always close on themselves even though the closure may not show within the confines of the map.
2. Contour lines of different elevations never touch except in the case of a vertical wall.
3. Contour lines never cross except where there is an overhanging cliff. Here the contours under the overhang should be dashed.
4. The contours of natural ground are usually curved and seldom have abrupt changes. They should be drawn freehand.
5. On plane surfaces, as in parking lots, the contour lines are straight. If the slope is even, the contours will be parallel and evenly spaced.
6. Contour lines are perpendicular to ridge and valley lines.

Though contours are used primarily to illustrate existing topographic conditions, "contour grading" can be used to show proposed finished contours. During preliminary stages of design, the contours as they will exist when the construction is complete can be drawn as a graphic illustration of the concept.

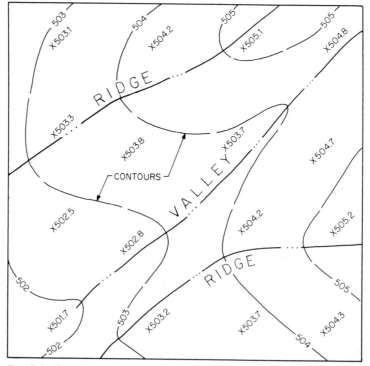

Fig. 5-2 Contours are lines connecting points of equal elevation. Elevations are shown at crosses.

Exact contours can be drawn during the design phase to be used for earthwork calculations and to show drainage patterns.

Setting Pad Elevations

The grading plan must be designed with an understanding of the drainage and roadway criteria presented in Chap. 6 and 8 of this book. The storm drainage and overall design are integrated with the grading plan.

On hilly or complicated sites, the first step may be a preliminary contour grading plan. Usually the street profiles can be designed as described in Chap. 6 and the top of curb elevations calculated and transferred to the grading plan. On residential and simple commercial industrial sites, the elevations of the pads should be selected so that they will drain to the front of the property. This will save the complications of draining storm water over adjacent properties.

The Federal Housing Administration describes three types of residential lot grading plans.

Type A. All the overland drainage on the lot is directed to the street at the front of the lot.

Type B. Drainage on the front half of the lot is directed to the street in front, and drainage on the back of the lot is directed to a street, alley, or ditch in the back of the lot.

Type C. All drainage is directed to the back of the lot.

Some jurisdictions allow only Type A drainage. Where Type B or C is allowed, remember that a ditch or other drainage facility must be designed for the back of the lot and that storm drainage easements must be acquired. All lots crossed with a ditch or underground system for storm drainage must be provided with a private storm drainage easement. On hillside sites where much of the site will be left natural, a ditch may be required at the property line to direct storm water falling on one site from crossing adjacent property.

Establishing the building pad elevations for single family residential lots is different from establishing pad elevations for commercial or industrial sites where parking lots are to be built.

Residential Pads

The criteria in selecting the residential pad elevations are:

1. The pad must be high enough above the lower top-of-curb elevation at the front of the property to accommodate a drainage swale around the house with a slope of at least 1 percent. Often the size of the lot and slope in the street are consistent, so a constant amount can be added to the lower top of the curb to establish adjacent pad elevations.
2. The pad must be designed so the grade on the driveway does not exceed 15 percent up (Fig. 5-3a) nor 10 percent down to the garage floor. The limiting cases are 15 and 10 percent. Flatter driveway slopes should be used wherever possible. A swale must be provided in the driveway in front of the garage

where the garage is below the street (Fig. 5-3*a*). When the building setback distance and driveway length are to be consistent in a subdivision, a consistent maximum elevation difference for a driveway down can be calculated. The elevation difference for a driveway up should be calculated using the top of the curb on the lower side of the driveway. The elevation difference for a driveway down should be calculated using the top of the curb on the

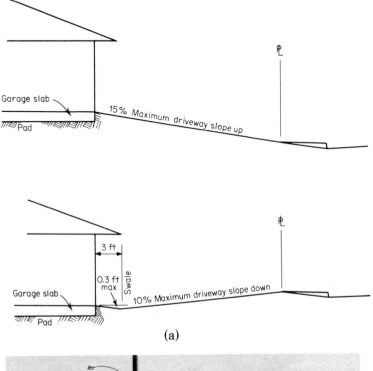

(a)

(b)

Fig. 5-3   (*a*) Driveway profiles. (*b*) Car on 12 percent driveway slope.

the higher side of the driveway. The driveway slope is a function of the length of driveway as well as the elevation difference. Where flexibility is allowed for the building setback, the driveway slope can be made less steep by making the driveway longer.

3. The widths of slopes between pads and surrounding features are affected by the vertical distances between them. Check that the slopes do not occupy so much space on adjacent lots that the level pad becomes too small to be useful.
4. Vertical differences between adjacent pads of less than 0.5 ft should be avoided. It is simpler to build three adjacent pads at one elevation and a fourth pad 0.6 ft different, than to build three pads each 0.2 ft different.

Commercial and Industrial Pads

The vertical location of building pads for commercial, industrial, and multifamily residential buildings must be coordinated with surrounding parking lots:

1. The pad must be determined so that the finished floor is above the high top of the curb. This is to prevent storm water from entering the building.
2. The storm water release point (Chap. 8) should not be more than 1.0 ft above the storm inlet.
3. The appearance of the building with respect to the street and other surroundings should be considered. If the building is much different in elevation from adjacent buildings and improvements, it will look out of place.

The building pad should be designed to extend beyond the building a distance recommended by the soils engineer. Usually, the minimum distance outside the foundation to provide room to work for construction equipment and personnel is 5 ft.

The pad elevation should be at least 0.2 ft higher than is necessary to satisfy the other criteria. If, during the course of construction, the earthwork does not balance, earth may have to be imported or exported. The cost in time and material of locating and importing earth usually exceeds the cost of exporting.

Take time to plan how the site can be designed differently, that is, which pads or areas can be built higher or lower if the site does not balance during construction. Prepare a table listing the size and location of these adjustments.

When designing the grading plan, care should be taken at the property boundaries. All necessary earth movement and slopes must not extend beyond the property lines unless a slope and/or construction easement has been acquired. If the profile of a street is in cut or fill, the street must be terminated far enough inside the property to allow for the slope to return to that of the natural ground at the property line (Fig. 5-4).

SOURCES OF EARTHWORK

There are several sources of earthwork activities that must be accounted for in designing and balancing the quantities of earthwork on a site.

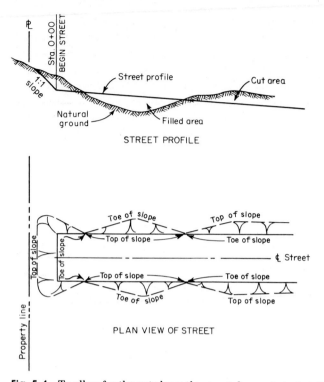

Fig. 5-4 To allow for the cut slope, the street does not start at the property line.

Unsuitable Material

Most sites have at least some material unsuitable for engineered fill. It may be debris dumped on the site from other sites, or it may be the naturally occurring top soil containing organic matter.

Organic material is unsuitable for compacted subbase and must be scraped from the site before construction of the base is begun. The depth of material to be removed should be recommended by the soils engineer. Even 0.25 ft of material to be removed over the entire site is significant and should be listed on the earthwork tabulation.

The organic material and soil is usually stockpiled on the site and used in finished grading and landscaping. If some is to be used on each lot, it will be most economical to stockpile on each lot to avoid the cost of transporting. If the soil is to be windrowed, be sure the windrow does not block overland flows.

Constructing the Base

The greatest source of earthwork is the cutting down of hills and filling in of valleys to create the level pads for buildings and moderate grades for roadbeds and channels.

Overcut and Overfill

Where buildings are to be built on the property line, the pad may have to be overcut or overfilled along side yards to provide space for workers and equipment (Fig. 5-5).

On residential sites, the entire lot may be built level at the rough grading stage. When the finished grading is done, a wedge-shaped section will be cut away from the pads above the street and filled in on pads below the street. These wedge-shaped areas are also referred to as areas of overcut or overfill and must be accounted for when listing the quantities of earth to be moved.

Trenches

The earth taken from trenches for utilities is called *trench spoil*. The trench is often then filled in with imported material providing special characteristics so the trench spoil is not replaced. This spoil is usually not significant in calculating earthwork for residential and commercial or industrial sites, but be aware that it is a significant factor on pipeline projects and may be a factor where unusually large trenches are required.

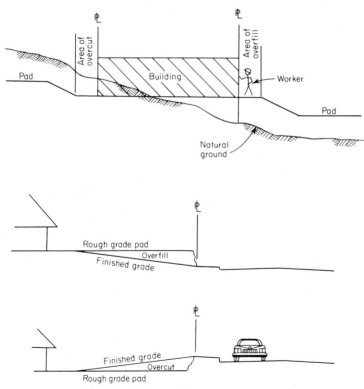

Fig. 5-5   Areas of overcut and overfill.

DETERMINING EARTHWORK QUANTITIES

There are three primary methods for determining earthwork quantities. Which is used depends upon the situation. They are averaging cut and fill depths, using cross sections, and using contour grading.

Averaging Cut and Fill Depths

The method that is the simplest, though least precise, is averaging cut and fill depths. This method is well suited to making quick, rough estimates of earthwork quantities. Its use is also indicated where the natural ground and shapes of lots are so uneven that the use of cross sections would be impractical.

If this method is to be used for residential lots, the corners of the lots are used. If the site is a quarry or waste disposal site or if the site is planned for commercial or industrial use without lots and streets, a grid is marked over the site at some convenient interval. The grid will create blocks. The size of blocks is arbitrary: 25 ft each way can be used for a small site, 100 ft for a large site. For residential sites, the earthwork quantity may be calculated for each lot. The streets would then be calculated separately.

The finished and existing elevations at each corner are read and marked on the plan. Differences in elevations and whether in cut or fill are then marked at each corner. Where there is a hump or depression within the area of the block, it should be marked as well. The four or more points are then averaged taking into account whether in cut or fill. This gives the average depth. It is then multiplied by the area in square feet. This yields cubic feet of cut or fill. Dividing the cubic feet by 27 ft³/yd³ gives cubic yards.

Where there are many blocks to calculate, a constant can be calculated representing the area divided by 27 ft³/yd³ and by the number of points averaged per lot to obtain the average depth. Care must be taken not to use the constant where more points are used because of a hump or depression within the block. By using the constant keyed into a memory slot of a calculator, the only procedure necessary to calculate the quantity of earthwork for each block is to enter and add algebraically the elevation differences and multiply that sum by the constant.

Example 5-2

Calculate the cubic yardage of cut or fill from Fig. 5-6.

Solution

Calculate a constant. The square footage of one square of a grid is 100 ft · 100 ft = 10,000 ft². There are four elevation points per grid.

$$10,000 \text{ ft}^2 \times \frac{1}{4 \text{ points}} \times \frac{\text{yd}^3}{27 \text{ ft}^3} = \frac{92.59 \text{ yd}^3}{\text{ft}}$$

Depths of cut will be given a positive sign. Depths of fill will be given a negative sign.

$$(-0.5) + (-1.4) + (0.5) + (-0.8) = -2.20 \text{ ft}$$

Quantity = K × average depth

$$\frac{92.59 \text{ yd}^3}{\text{ft}} \times (-2.20 \text{ ft}) = 203.7 \text{ yd}^3 \text{ fill}$$

It is not advisable to carry the quantities in the calculator for a summation. Write the quantity in each square so that a comparison between squares can be made. This way, errors can be easily observed. The quantities of the blocks will form a pattern or trend of increasing or decreasing values. Those blocks that do not conform to the trend should be suspect. If it is not clear from observation why those blocks do not fit the trend, the quantity should be recalculated.

Cross Sections

Streets, highways, and other linear structures such as canals and dikes are particularly well suited to the use of cross sections for calculation of earthwork

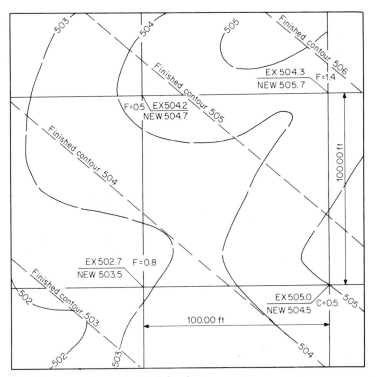

Fig. 5-6 Averaging cut and fill depths.

quantities. When commercial or industrial sites are constructed in even terrain, the use of cross sections is also indicated.

To successfully use cross sections to calculate earthwork quantities, locations of representative cross sections must be carefully chosen and the cross sections drawn perpendicular to the centerline or other reference line (Fig. 5-7). For linear structures, cross sections should be drawn at:

1. All high and low points of the natural ground.
2. Points where the profile crosses the natural ground; i.e., cut changes to fill, or fill changes to cut.
3. Points where the slope of the natural ground or the grade of the profile changes direction.
4. Changes in the natural ground not reflected on the profile.

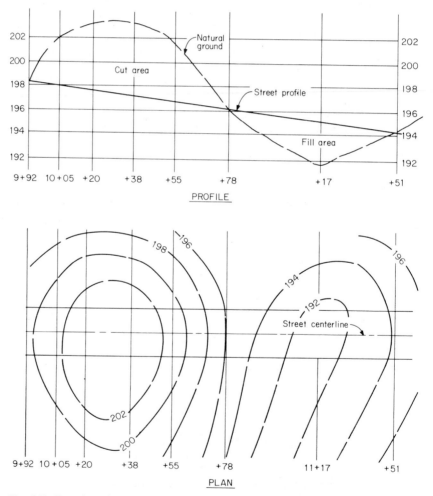

Fig. 5-7 Location of cross sections to use for earthwork quantities.

5. Places where there are changes in appurtenant structures, such as ditches or dikes, at the side of the main structure.

For site plans, sections should be drawn:

1. At property lines. Here the cut and/or fill should be zero, unless there is a vertical retaining wall.
2. Just before and just after paved sections.
3. Just before and just after building pads.
4. At high and low points in the streets or parking lots.

The cross sections should be drawn to scale on grid paper (Fig. 5-8). Any scale will work, and the vertical and horizontal scales may be the same, but it is not

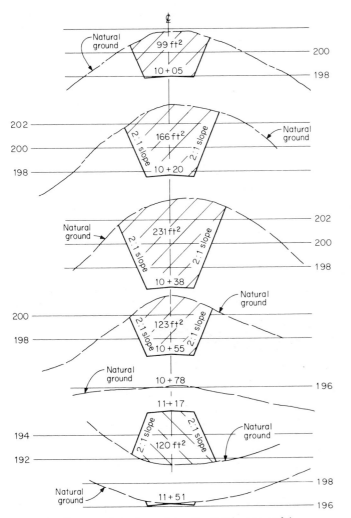

Fig. 5-8   Cross sections drawn from Fig. 5-7 (not to scale).

necessary. The drawing of cross sections is useful, not just for calculating earth-work quantities but as a visual aid to spotting trouble spots otherwise missed and for locating cut and fill catch points. Where the natural ground is at a slope near the designed slope for new construction, the cut or fill slope may not "catch" within the right-of-way or within a reasonable distance. In this case, a retaining wall or other design is indicated. The cross section should include the natural or existing groundline and a cross section of the proposed structure.

For the purpose of earthwork, the cross section can be represented in more than one way. For example, a line can be drawn across the top of the roadbed. A straight line can be drawn from hinge point to hinge point or from the top of the curb to the top of the curb (Fig. 5-9). The earthwork is then calculated as cut or fill to that line, and the net cut for the street section is subtracted. Another way is to draw a template below the aggregate base, and calculate the earthwork from the template. Using the template provides the earthwork without the additional step of subtracting the street section.

When representative cross sections have been drawn, the areas enclosed must be measured or calculated. The areas can be divided into trapezoids and triangles and their areas calculated, or a planimeter can be used to measure the areas. Use of a planimeter is preferable because it is faster.

The planimeter (Fig. 5-10) is an instrument for measuring plane surfaces. It is L shaped. One arm is equipped with a pushpin to secure it to the drawing being measured. The other arm has a pointer disk and graduated cylinder to indicate the area measured. The arms are hinged to swing freely.

To use the planimeter:

1. Place the drawing to be measured on a flat, level surface with no papers or other objects beneath to interrupt the smooth tracing of the area.

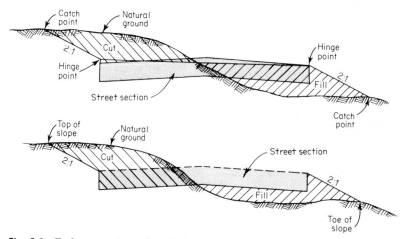

Fig. 5-9   End-area cross sections for earthwork quantities.

2. Place the static point (pushpin) so the arms form as near a 90° angle as possible when tracing the area. When the arm is extended, the measurement loses accuracy. Break the area into smaller areas if necessary.
3. Set the dials at zero.
4. Trace the area freehand with the pointer. When tracing is done freehand, the pointer will move inside and outside the line and the movements will compensate, but if a straight edge is used, the whole line will be inside or outside the true location, creating a cumulative error.
5. Always trace the area twice. Note the area the first time and verify that tracing the area twice yields twice the value. This is a simple check to guard against not having the dials set at zero at the beginning.

Fig. 5-10 Planimeter.

The planimeter will have a graduated disk and a graduated cylinder from which to read the area. Read the disk first. This figure is in tens of inches. Read inches from the cylinder. The graduations between inches indicate tenths of inches. Hundredths of inches can be read from the vernier side of the cylinder.

The planimeter shows square inches measured. Some plainimeters have an adjustable arm that, when adjusted precisely, will compensate for the scales used, so square feet can be read directly. Unless the same scale is always used with the planimeter, this flexibility introduces a source of error, and since it is simple to calculate a constant to convert square inches to square feet, use of an adjustable arm is discouraged for this purpose.

Example 5-3

Calculate the area of a cross section. The scale used is 1 in = 10 ft horizontal, 1 in = 1 ft vertical. Use Fig. 5-11 to read square inches.

Solution

The planimeter reads 23.15 in^2.

$$\text{The scale} = \frac{10 \text{ ft}}{1 \text{ in horiz.}} \times \frac{1 \text{ ft}}{1 \text{ in vert.}} = \frac{10 \text{ ft}^2}{\text{in}^2}$$

$$\frac{10 \text{ ft}^2}{\text{in}^2} \times 23.15 \text{ in}^2 = 231.5 \text{ ft}^2$$

When all the cross-sectional areas have been measured and their values written on the cross sections, examine each compared with the others. Is the measured value of the largest area the largest number? Does the smallest visible area have the smallest measured area? Does one area that appears to be twice as large as another measure twice as large? By examining the results critically, you may be able to discover errors.

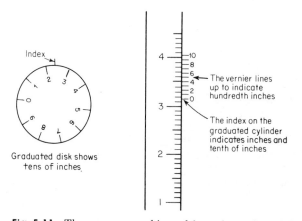

Fig. 5-11   The area measured is read from the graduated disk and cylinder on the planimeter.

When areas have been determined for each section, the volume can be determined using the average end-area formula, shown in Eq. 5-2.

$$V = \frac{A_1 + A_2}{2} L \qquad\qquad (5\text{-}2)$$

where V = volume, ft^3
A_1, A_2 = end areas, ft^2
L = distance between end areas, ft

This formula gives the volume of earth in cubic feet between two cross sections. The volume must be divided by 27 ft^3/yd^3 to acquire cubic yards. The sum of the volumes between all the cross sections is the volume for the site.

To facilitate the calculation, use the Earthwork Calculations Form (Fig. 5-12). To fill out the form and perform calculations for the volume, follow the steps listed below.

1. Write in the stations. There should be a station at the beginning of project or property line, and at the end of project or property line.
2. Enter the areas of cut in column 2, and the areas of fill in column 6 opposite their stations. The areas can be entered as square feet, or the planimeter reading in square inches may be used if a conversion factor from square inches to square feet is included in the value of $K\left(K = \frac{1}{2} \times \frac{1 \text{ yd}^3}{27 \text{ ft}^3} \times \frac{\text{ft}^2}{\text{in}^2} \right).$
3. Determine the distances between the stations, and enter them in column 4 where there is cut and column 8 where there is fill.
4. Add the areas (column 2) of the first[2] and second station and enter the result in column 3 between the two stations.
5. Add the areas at the second and third station, and enter the result in column 3 between those two stations.
6. Continue until all adjacent areas have been added and entered on the form.
7. Perform steps 4 through 6 for area in fill, filling in columns.
8. Multiply columns 3 and 4 and K. Enter the volume in column 5.
9. Multiply columns 7 and 8 and K. Enter the volume in column 9.
10. Total column 5. The sum is the total volume of cut.
11. Total column 9. The sum is the total volume of fill.

The earthwork volume for the cross sections in Figs. 5-7 and 5-8 is calculated using the form shown in Fig. 5-13.

Contour Grading

Drawing the contours for a proposed project is called *contour grading*. To the trained eye, contour grading provides a visual, plan view representation of how the finished product will look and how drainage will work.

---

[2]The first and last station should always have zero area unless they are at vertical retaining walls.

Contour grading can also be used to determine earthwork quantities. Complicated projects in irregular terrain may require contour grading, if there is little room for error in determining earthwork quantities.

Drawing contours of a proposed project requires ability for abstract thinking and three-dimensional visualization. One technique that can help on linear projects is to draw profiles of the break points in the cross sections. The stations at which these profiles cross even elevations can then be taken from the profile

EARTHWORK CALCULATIONS FORM

		Cut				Fill		
(1) Station	(2) Area	(3) Double end area	(4) Length	(5) Volume K·(3)·(4)	(6) Area	(7) Double end area	(8) Length	(9) Volume K·(7)·(8)

Fig. 5-12 Earthwork calculations form.

and plotted on the plan view in the correct relation to the reference line. When all the points of that elevation are plotted, they can then be connected. Where the project is on an even grade, the contours will be at even intervals and parallel. In horizontal and vertical curves, the contours will be curved (Fig. 5-14*a* and *b*). When drawing proposed contours on nonlinear projects, mark elevations at all break points and interpolate the locations for the contours as described earlier in the section on contours.

EARTHWORK CALCULATIONS FORM

(1) Station	(2) Area	(3) Double end area	(4) Length	(5) Volume $K \cdot (3) \cdot (4)$	(6) Area	(7) Double end area	(8) Length	(9) Volume $K \cdot (7) \cdot (8)$
		Cut				Fill		
9 + 92	0							
		99	13	23				
10 + 05	99							
		265	15	73				
+ 20	166							
		397	18	132				
+ 38	231							
		354	17	111				
+ 55	123							
		123	23	52				
+ 78	0				0			
						120	39	87
11 + 17					120			
						120	34	76
+ 51					0			
		Total cut		391 yd³		Total fill		163 yd³
		$K = \frac{1}{2} \times$	$\frac{yd^3}{27\ ft^3}$	$= \frac{yd^3}{54\ ft^3}$				

Fig. 5-13 Earthwork calculations form filled out.

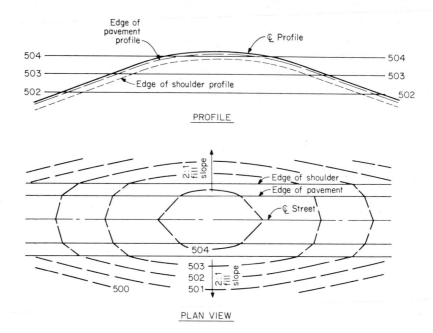

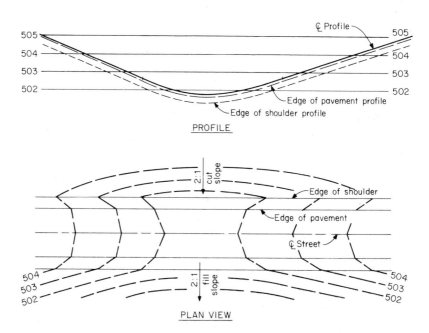

Fig. 5-14 (*a*) Contour grading of crest curve. (*b*) Contour grading of sag curve.

86

The proposed contours should connect with existing contours of equal elevation at the catch point (top of slope or toe of slope). When the project is built, the new contour will start at the catch point on one side of the project, follow the proposed contour through the new area, and connect to the old contour at the catch point on the other side of the project. The old contour between catch points will cease to exist (Fig. 5-15).

Earthwork volumes can be calculated using the new contour and that portion of the old contour to be obliterated by the project. Plane areas enclosed by the proposed and existing contours are measured with the planimeter for each elevation. Tracing the perimeter enclosed by the proposed and existing contour of each elevation in a different color helps delineate the area, as the proposed contour may cross several existing contours (Fig. 5-16). The volume is then calculated in the same manner and using the same form as for cross sections. Column 1 becomes contour elevations, and columns 4 and 8 will be the contour interval. When columns 4 and 8 do not change—a consistent contour interval is used—their value can be included in the constant used in columns 5 and 9.

Balancing the Earthwork

When the cut and fill quantities have been calculated and tabulated, the total cut and fill should be compared. It is desirable for the cut and fill quantities, including the shrinkage factor, to be equal. The earthwork is then said to balance. When the earthwork does not balance, the plane of part or all of the site

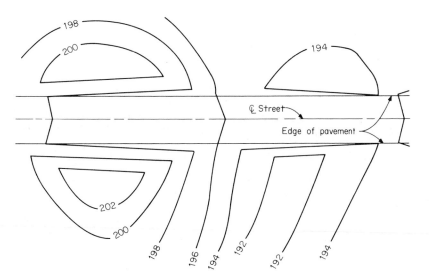

Fig. 5-15 Final contours from Fig. 5-16.

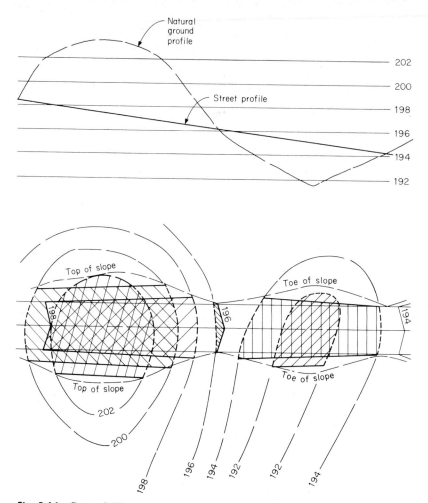

Fig. 5-16   Cut and fill areas for calculating earthwork from contour grading.

should be raised or lowered until the site does balance. This will require some recalculation of grades next to the property boundaries. Earthwork quantities, including quantities allowing for shrinkage, will have to be recalculated. This redesign and recalculation may have to be done more than once.

To estimate the size of the change to be made, convert the excess or shortage of material to cubic feet by multiplying the cubic yardage by 27 ft^3/yd^3. Then divide the cubic feet by the square footage of the site or area to be adjusted. The result will be the depth of material necessary to balance the earthwork spread evenly over the site.

Example 5-4

The earthwork for a site of $43,000$ ft^2 has the following earthwork tabulation.

	Cut, yd^3	Fill, yd^3
Pads and parking	4780	2800
Compaction (25%)		700
Organic material	320	
Stockpile for landscaping		320
Total	5100	3820

How much should the site be raised or lowered?

Solution

1. Calculate the difference between cut and fill totals. $5100 - 3820 = 1280$ yd^3.
2. Convert to cubic feet.

$$1280 \text{ yd}^3 \times 27 \text{ ft}^3/\text{yd}^3 = 34{,}560 \text{ ft}^3$$

3. Divide the excess material by the area of the site.

$$34{,}560 \text{ ft}^3 \div 43{,}000 \text{ ft}^2 = 0.8 \text{ ft}$$

At this point redraw the cross sections 0.8 ft higher, remeasure the areas, and recalculate the quantities. The cut, fill, and compaction quantities will all change. It is unlikely that the site will balance after the first redesign because the locations of change from cut to fill will change and because the adjustment should diminish to zero at the project boundaries. With each redesign, verify that the driveway slopes and other criteria, outlined earlier, continue to be satisfied.

THE GRADING PLAN

All the information the grading contractor will need should be shown on the grading plan (Fig. 5-17). It should be completely independent of the rest of the plans for the site. The grading plan base map should be made on a topography map and drawn to scale. It is useful to have the topography map "screened" photographically. In the screening process, a photographic procedure screens out some of the density of the lines, so they will appear to be faded. The property boundary, lot, and easement lines are then drawn on the screened copy. This way the topographic information is available and serves as a background on which to present the plan. The plan should show a typical section or sections for the pads and for the streets with slopes and setback distances from property

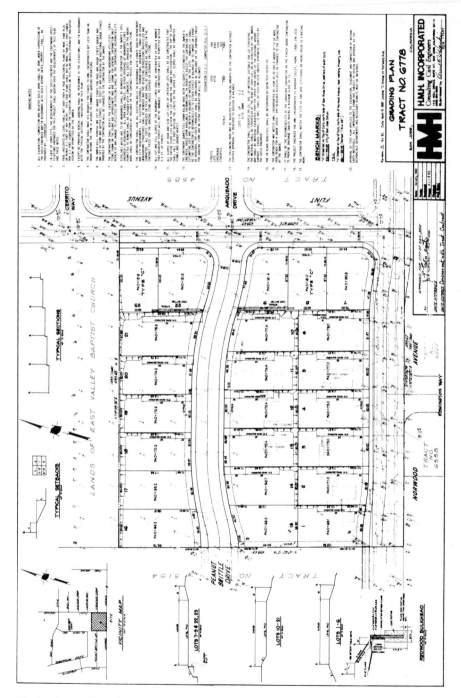

Fig. 5-17 Grading plan.

90

lines and/or buildings. Cross sections for ditches, dikes, and other drainage structures that are an integral part of the plan and will be the responsibility of the grading contractor should be shown.

The areas of fill should be shaded or otherwise delineated differently from areas of cut to show the extent of transporting earth around the site.

An important part of the plan is the notes. The notes should include the name of the soils engineer, project engineer, and jurisdictional agency. A table of the cut and fill quantities and a table of alternate locations for adjustments should be given (note 13, Fig. 5-17). Descriptions of how to handle special problems, such as underground tanks, should be given. If erosion control measures are to be taken, they should be described in the notes and details. A check list for grading plans is included as Fig. 5-18.

GRADING PLAN CHECKLIST
a. Existing topography
b. Vicinity map
c. North arrow
d. Property boundaries; bearings and distances
e. Lots and blocks or parcels, easements; distances
f. Street names
g. Bench mark
h. Title block
i. Typical sections
j. Top of curb elevations
k. Pad elevations. Areas of cut or fill should be shaded on large projects.
l. Slopes
m. Ditches
n. Bulkheads or retaining walls
o. Details
p. Notes

Fig. 5-18 Grading plan checklist.

Chapter Six

Streets and Parking Lots

In designing streets and roads, the primary consideration is to provide a safe, smooth, and comfortable ride. This fact applies whether the traveled way is a major highway or a neighborhood street. The primary difference in the design considerations for rural roads and for city streets is that city streets are typically an integral part of the storm drainage system. Though storm drainage is an important consideration that must be planned for on rural roads, it has far less influence on design.

HORIZONTAL ALIGNMENT

In open country, the horizontal location of a road is determined by the shortest route between two points, the alignment that requires the least earthwork, the stopping and passing sight distances, and the preservation of natural resources. In locating a street in a new subdivision, the way that street divides the property relative to the lots it delineates is the predominant criterion. In an existing urban area, avoidance of expensive property must predominate.

Establishing the Centerline

Streets and roads must have a centerline or other line to which their various elements can be referenced. On simple streets the centerline is ordinarily used. On roads where the opposing traveled ways are separated and on one-way ramps, the axis of rotation (Fig. 6-20) is usually most convenient. As long as the location of the reference line is clear, the reference line can be anywhere. For simplicity, the centerline will be the reference line in this book.

The location of the centerline of a street must be established relative to its legal environment. The way to accomplish this is with a bearing and distance from a known point. Usually the location is measured along a property line from a property corner. From there, the courses of the centerline are described with bearings and distances. The centerline is tied to other known points where it crosses property lines or streets. Where centerlines cross, stationing equations, described below, are given. Where the centerline changes direction, a tangent, circular curve is inserted for a smooth transition. The geometric relationships of circular curves are illustrated in Fig. 6-1. The radius, the central angle, and the length are all that is necessary to describe the curve. This information should be shown on the plans either next to the curve or on a table. The radius and deflection (Δ) are usually known or are set during design. When the radius or deflection is not known, the equations given in Fig. 6-1 can be manipulated algebraically to give a value for either one.

The centerline is stationed. *Stationing* is simply marking the distance every 100 ft. The stations are numbered consecutively starting with 0 at some convenient location, such as the tract boundary or a street intersection. The sta-

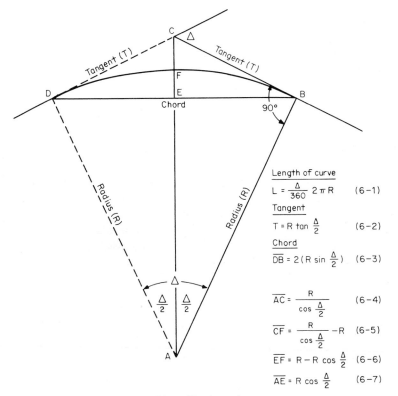

Length of curve
$$L = \frac{\Delta}{360}\, 2\pi R \qquad (6\text{-}1)$$

Tangent
$$T = R \tan \frac{\Delta}{2} \qquad (6\text{-}2)$$

Chord
$$\overline{DB} = 2\left(R \sin \frac{\Delta}{2}\right) \qquad (6\text{-}3)$$

$$\overline{AC} = \frac{R}{\cos \frac{\Delta}{2}} \qquad (6\text{-}4)$$

$$\overline{CF} = \frac{R}{\cos \frac{\Delta}{2}} - R \qquad (6\text{-}5)$$

$$\overline{EF} = R - R \cos \frac{\Delta}{2} \qquad (6\text{-}6)$$

$$\overline{AE} = R \cos \frac{\Delta}{2} \qquad (6\text{-}7)$$

Fig. 6-1　Geometric relationships of horizontal curves.

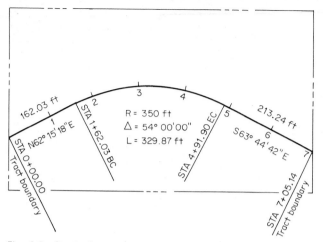

Fig. 6-2 Stationing a curve.

tions are labeled as $1+00$, $2+00$, $3+00$. . . . Where the station or a measurement is needed at a point some distance other than an even 100 ft, the station
is given as station plus feet and hundredths of a foot. The station $1+32.66$ is
132.66 ft from the $0+00$ station. It is desirable for the stationing to run from
left to right on the plans whenever possible.

The bearings and distances of the centerline are calculated and then labeled
in degrees, minutes, and seconds and in feet and hundredths of a foot, respec-
tively. Wherever there are curves, the radii, central angles (delta), and lengths
of the curves must be calculated. This information is all that is needed to station the streets. This is illustrated in Fig. 6-2. Here the centerline distance from
the tract boundary (sta $0+00$) to the beginning of the curve (BC) is calculated
to be 162.03 ft, the length of the curve is 329.87 ft, and the centerline distance
from the end of the curve (EC) to the other tract boundary is calculated to be
213.24 ft. The BC station is $1+62.03$, the EC station is $4+91.90$, and the station
at the tract boundary is $7+05.14$.

In some circumstances, a stationing equation is needed. For example it is
needed when the center of northbound and southbound lanes are separated
with a median and the distance between them is to be made narrower, or when
the street width changes in a way that the centerlines or curbs are not parallel,
concentric, nor symmetrical with respect to the centerline. Another example of
this is where portions of an old road are redesigned so that the stationing
changes back and forth between new and existing.

Example 6-1

Determine the stationing equation at the EC of the new centerline of Winding Road
as illustrated in Fig. 6-3. Use equations in Fig. 6-1.

Solution

1. We see from the illustration that the centerlines coincide except for the portion within the curves. Therefore, we know that the central angle of each curve is the same. We know from geometry that curves with different radii and the same central angle have different curve lengths and tangent lengths.

2. Calculate the tangent length of the existing curves and the new curves using $T = R \tan (\Delta/2)$ (Eq. 6-2). First calculate $\Delta/2$.

$$\frac{\Delta}{2} = \frac{83° \ 40'}{2}$$

$$83° = 82° + 60'$$

$$\begin{array}{r} 82° + 60' \\ + \ 40' \\ \hline 82° \ 100' \end{array}$$

$$\frac{82°}{2} + \frac{100'}{2} = 41° \ 50'$$

$$\frac{83° \ 40'}{2} = 41° \ 50'$$

The tangent of 41° 50′ is 0.8951506.

$$T_{\text{new}} = 370 \text{ ft} \times 0.8951506 \doteq 331.21 \text{ ft}$$
$$T_{\text{existing}} = 225 \text{ ft} \times 0.8951506 = 201.41 \text{ ft}$$

3. Calculate the difference of tangent lengths.

$$331.21 \text{ ft} - 201.41 \text{ ft} = 129.80 \text{ ft}$$

4. Subtract the difference of tangent lengths (129.80 ft) from the BC station of the existing centerline.*

*Note: In equations, station numbers are given in parentheses to distinguish them from lengths.

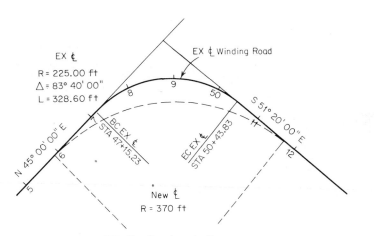

Fig. 6-3 Existing Winding Road centerline.

$$(47+15.23) - 129.80 \text{ ft} = (45+85.43)$$

This is the station of the BC of the new centerline.

5. Calculate the length of the curve of the new centerline. Use Eq. 6-1. First convert degrees, minutes, and seconds to degrees and decimals of degrees.

$$\frac{40'}{60'/\text{degree}} = 0.667°$$

$$83° \ 40' = 83.67°$$

$$L = \frac{\Delta}{360°} 2\pi R$$

$$= \frac{83.67°}{360°} \times 2 \times \pi \times 370 \text{ ft}$$

$$= 540.32 \text{ ft}$$

6. Determine the station of the new EC.

$$\text{Sta new BC} + \text{length of new curve} = \text{new EC}$$
$$(45+85.43) + 540.32 \text{ ft} = (51+25.75)$$

7. Determine where the new EC becomes tangent to the old centerline. Add the tangent difference (129.80 ft) to the EC of the existing centerline.

$$(50+43.83) + 129.80 \text{ ft} = (51+73.63)$$

The equation is

$$\text{EC sta } 51+25.75 \text{ new} = \text{POT Ex sta } 51+73.63$$

The new centerline will be 47.83 ft shorter than the old one (Fig. 6-4).

When you calculate the slopes along conduits or along curbs and gutters in curves, care must be taken not to use the difference of stationing as the length of the curb or conduit. The length of the curb must be measured or calculated

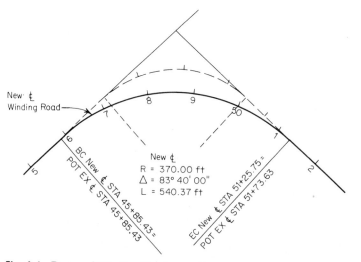

Fig. 6-4 Proposed Winding Road centerline.

from the plan view. The length of a curve will be shorter than the centerline when it is concentric with and *inside* the centerline curve. It will be longer when it is concentric with and *outside* the centerline curve. The formula for calculating the length of a curve not on the centerline is the same as it is for the centerline (Eq. 6-1). The only factor that is different is the radius.

$$L_{CL} = \frac{\Delta}{360°} 2\pi R_{CL} \qquad L_{CRB} = \frac{\Delta}{360°} 2\pi R_{CRB}$$

$$\frac{L_{CL}}{R_{CL}} = \frac{\Delta}{360°} 2\pi \qquad \frac{L_{CRB}}{R_{CRB}} = \frac{\Delta}{360°} 2\pi$$

$$\frac{L_{CL}}{R_{CL}} = \frac{L_{CRB}}{R_{CRB}}$$

A constant can be calculated for the relationship L_{CL}/R_{CL}. This constant can then be used to easily calculate the lengths of all other lines that are concentric with the centerline.

$$\frac{L_{CL}}{R_{CL}} = K \tag{6-8}$$

$$K = \frac{L_{CRB}}{R_{CRB}} \tag{6-9}$$

$$K \times R_{CRB} = L_{CRB} \tag{6-10}$$

Example 6-2

Calculate the length of the right curb between sta 5+00 and 8+92.70 from Fig. 6-5.

Solution

1. Calculate a constant for the relationship of the centerline radius and the length of the centerline curve.

$$\frac{L_{CL}}{R_{CL}} = \frac{392.70 \text{ ft}}{500.00 \text{ ft}} = 0.7854 = K \tag{6-8}$$

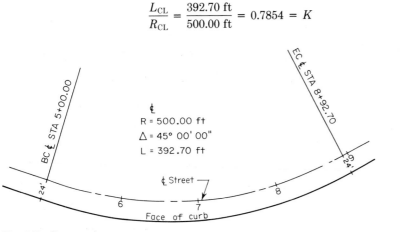

Fig. 6-5 Concentric curves.

2. Calculate the radius of the right curb.

$$500.00 \text{ ft} + 24.00 \text{ ft} = 524.00 \text{ ft} = R_{CRB}$$

3. Calculate the length of the right curb.

$$\begin{aligned} L_{CRB} &= K \times R_{CRB} \\ &= 0.7854 \times 524.00 \text{ ft} \\ &= 411.55 \text{ ft} \end{aligned} \qquad (6\text{-}10)$$

A precise length of the curve is necessary for calculations of quantities and where the slopes are near the minimum allowable for adequate flows.

Horizontal Sight Distances

The distance required for a driver, traveling at a given speed, to bring his or her car to a stop after sighting an object in the road is called the *stopping sight distance.*

On a horizontal curve, the stopping sight distance is measured as the line of sight (a straight line) from one point on the curve to another. The line of sight forms a chord of the curve. The area enclosed within the curve and the line of sight must be kept clear of obstructions (Fig. 6-6). The approval agency will dictate minimum radii to be used for curves and distances from the curves for which the line of sight must be preserved.

VERTICAL ALIGNMENT

The half of the plan sheet used for the longitudinal, vertical design of the street and utilities is called the *profile.* It will show the natural ground and the street profile at the centerline. The profiles of sewers and other utilities will be projected into the vertical plane of the centerline. Other information necessary or helpful for designing the profiles should also be shown.

The stationing of the centerline will be shown on the profile. When calculating slopes for other features of the profile, care must be taken not to use the difference of stationing as the length of the conduit or curb when the centerline alignment is a curve.

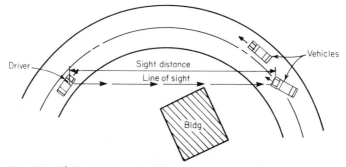

Fig. 6-6 Horizontal stopping sight distance.

Designing the Street Profile

When the street to be designed is longer than will fit on one plan sheet, the use of profile paper is recommended. If you use profile paper long enough for the entire street and select the vertical scale to accommodate the fall from one end of the street to the other, the profile can be shown without breaks. Draw the natural ground at the centerline, and show the existing profiles of the streets to be connected to or crossed. Features that may affect the alignment, such as existing underground utilities, trees to be saved within the right-of-way, or overhead power lines, should be plotted and their elevations shown.

In subdivisions where adjacent lots must be drained to the street, the profile should be set low enough to allow drainage from the lots. On lots 100 ft deep and 50 ft wide, the overland flow will have to travel half the width plus the length of the lot [(50/2)+100 = 125 ft]. At 1 percent fall for 125 ft the street should be located vertically so that the highest top-of-curb elevation at the property line is at least 1.25 ft (125 ft $\times$ 0.01) below the pad elevations.

When a road is to be located in open country, the profile should be located so that the drainage flows away from the road laterally. When necessary, drainage ditches will transport storm water away from the road. If the road is located in hilly or mountainous terrain, balancing earthwork becomes an important criterion.

The street or road profile should follow the slope of the natural ground as much as possible. The more closely it follows the ground, the less earthwork will be required. Where changes in the natural grade occur, a change should be made in the slope of the street profile. By putting your eye next to the paper, at one end of the profile, the location of the angle point in the slope of the natural ground becomes apparent. Judgment must be exercised as to how closely to follow the natural ground. Too many grade breaks result in an unsafe, uncomfortable ride and increased engineering and surveying costs.

The profile must allow enough vertical clearance to allow for culverts or other drainage facilities and must be coordinated with other existing and proposed surface, subsurface, and overhead conditions and improvements. In hilly terrain, the natural ground will be used only as a guide to locating the profile. Balancing the amounts of excavation and fill is a more important consideration.

Calculating the Profile

Once a profile for the street has been designed visually, its location must be calculated. The elevation of the point on the existing street where the new street begins should be known from the topographic survey. It is not sufficient to simply use, from existing plans, the elevations of centerlines and tops of curb to be met. A survey crew must locate existing centerline elevations to within 0.01 ft vertically at the line of intersection of the proposed and existing streets and at 25-ft intervals and at grade breaks back along the existing street for 50 to 100 ft behind the connection. This information will provide the existing slopes. To provide a smooth transition, keep the slope of the proposed street within 2 percent of the existing slope. If a change of slope greater than 2 percent is needed, a vertical curve should be provided in the profile. This may require the removal of some of the existing street.

Write on the profile the elevation at the connection and the slope projected from that connection. The approximate elevation of the next grade break can be measured directly from the profile, and a slope for that section of the street can be determined.

The slope is calculated by dividing the horizontal difference between break points into the vertical (elevation) difference between the same points.

Example 6-3

Calculate the slope between sta 10+00 and sta 18+00 from Fig. 6-7.

Solution

1. Calculate the distance between sta 10+00 and sta 18+00.

$$(18+00) - (10+00) = 800 \text{ ft}$$

2. Calculate the difference in elevation between sta 10+00 and sta 18+00.

$$121.62 \text{ ft} - 117.26 \text{ ft} = 4.36 \text{ ft}$$

3. The slope is the elevation difference divided by the distance between stations.

$$4.36 \text{ ft} \div 800 \text{ ft} = 0.00545$$

The slope is 0.00545. Slopes are sometimes expressed as percentages. This slope would be 0.545 percent. The slope is said to be negative because it is going downhill.

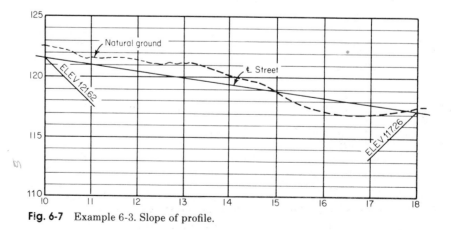

Fig. 6-7   Example 6-3. Slope of profile.

This process can also be reversed. When the slope and the elevation at one station is available, the unknown elevation at another station can be calculated.

Example 6-4

Given an elevation of 121.62 at sta 10+00 and a slope of -0.00545, calculate the elevation at sta 15+30.54.

Solution

1. Calculate the distance between stations.

$$(15+30.54) - (10+00) = 530.54 \text{ ft}$$

2. Multiply the slope times the distance.

$$-0.00545 \times 530.54 \text{ ft} = -2.89 \text{ ft}$$

This gives the vertical difference in elevations. To get the elevation at sta 15+30.54, add the difference algebraically to the elevation at sta 10+00.

$$121.62 \text{ ft} + (-2.89 \text{ ft}) = 118.73 \text{ ft}$$
118.73 is the elevation at sta 15+30.54.

When the slope of conduits change on gravity-flow storm and sanitary sewer lines, a manhole is added at the grade break. When the slope of the street grade changes more than 2 percent, a vertical curve should be used. The length of the vertical curve used is determined by passing and stopping sight distances. These are discussed below.

The vertical curves used for streets, and sometimes sewers, are parabolic curves. Deriving the formulas for parabolic curves requires an understanding of calculus. Fortunately, however, all that is needed to calculate and plot vertical curves are three simple equations (Fig. 6-8).

When the profile goes from a positive (uphill) slope to a negative (downhill) slope, from positive slope to a flatter positive slope, or from a negative slope to a steeper negative slope, the curve used is said to be a *crest curve* (Fig. 6-9). When the profile goes from a negative slope to a positive slope, from a negative to a flatter negative slope, or from a positive slope to a steeper positive slope, the curve is called a *sag curve*. The highest point on a crest curve and the lowest point on a sag curve are called the *critical point*. Sag curves form bowls. Crest curves form inverted bowls. When the slopes are equal in value but opposite in direction, the critical point will fall at the station of the *point of intersection* (PI) of the grades. When grades change but both are positive or both are negative, the critical point falls at one end.

The critical point on sag curves is particularly important because it determines where drainage facilities must be located.

To lay out smooth vertical curves, elevations should be calculated at the critical point and at the midpoint—or more frequently if necessary. Construction

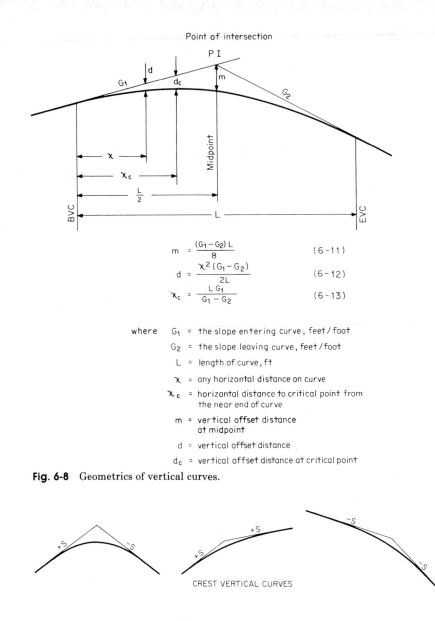

$$m = \frac{(G_1 - G_2) L}{8} \qquad (6-11)$$

$$d = \frac{x^2 (G_1 - G_2)}{2L} \qquad (6-12)$$

$$x_c = \frac{L G_1}{G_1 - G_2} \qquad (6-13)$$

where
G_1 = the slope entering curve, feet / foot

G_2 = the slope leaving curve, feet / foot

L = length of curve, ft

x = any horizontal distance on curve

x_c = horizontal distance to critical point from the near end of curve

m = vertical offset distance at midpoint

d = vertical offset distance

d_c = vertical offset distance at critical point

Fig. 6-8 Geometrics of vertical curves.

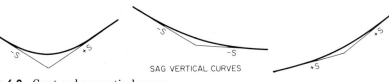

CREST VERTICAL CURVES

SAG VERTICAL CURVES

Fig. 6-9 Crest and sag vertical curves.

102

stakes should be no more than 50 ft apart. Plotting the curve on the plan and profile sheet is done with french curves. The curve should be tangent at the beginning of the vertical curve (BVC) and at the end of the vertical curve (EVC) and should go through three elevation points.

Example 6-5

Given Figs. 6-8 and 6-10, calculate the elevation at the midpoint of the curve and the location and elevation to place catch basins between sta $23+20$ and sta $27+00$. Use a 320-ft vertical curve.

Solution

1. The center of the curve will be at the PI, sta $25+00$. The BVC will be located back of the PI by half the length of the vertical curve.

$$320 \text{ ft} \div 2 = 160 \text{ ft}$$
$$\text{BVC sta} = (25+00) - 160 \text{ ft} = (23+40)$$
$$\text{EVC sta} = (23+40) + 320 \text{ ft} = (26+60)$$

2. Calculate the elevation at the PI.
    a. Determine the distance between a station of known elevation $(23+20)$ and the PI station.

$$(25+00) - (23+20) = 180 \text{ ft}$$

    b. Multiply the distance by the slope.

$$180 \text{ ft} (-0.05) = -9.00 \text{ ft}$$

    c. Add algebraically the vertical difference to the known elevation.

$$276.32 \text{ ft} + (-9.00 \text{ ft}) = 267.32 \text{ ft}$$

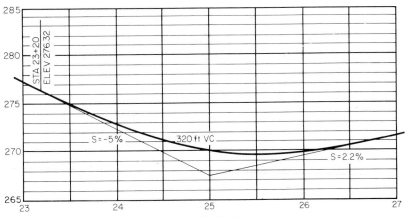

Fig. 6-10 Example 6-5. Locating the critical point.

3. Calculate the vertical offset distance at the midpoint.

$$m = \frac{(G_1 - G_2)L}{8}$$
$$= \frac{(-0.05 - 0.022)320 \text{ ft}}{8} \qquad (6\text{-}11)$$
$$= 2.88 \text{ ft}$$

This is a sag curve, so the elevation on the midpoint of the curve is the elevation at the PI plus the m distance. On crest curves the m distance is subtracted from the PI.

$$267.32 \text{ ft} + 2.88 \text{ ft} = 270.20 \text{ ft}$$

The elevation on the curve at the midpoint is 270.20.

4. Calculate the location and elevation of the critical point.
   a. Determine the distance from the near end of the curve to the critical point. It can be seen from Fig. 6-10 that the critical point will lie between sta 25+00 and the EVC.

   To calculate the critical point in that area, G_1 will be 0.022 (2.2 percent) and will be negative as viewed from the end of the curve nearest the critical point. G_2 will be 0.05 (5 percent) and will be positive as viewed from the end of the curve nearest the critical point. Use Eq. 6-10.

$$\chi_c = \frac{LG_1}{G_1 - G_2}$$
$$= \frac{320(-0.022)}{-0.022 - 0.05} \qquad (6\text{-}13)$$
$$= 97.78 \text{ ft}$$

The critical point is 97.78 ft from the EVC. The station of the critical point is

$$\text{EVC sta } 26+60 - 97.78 \text{ ft} = \text{sta } 25+62.22$$

   b. Calculate the elevation at the critical point. The elevation on the tangent must be calculated first.

$$(25+62.22) - (25+00) = 62.22 \text{ ft}$$
$$267.32 \text{ ft} + 62.24 \text{ ft}(0.022) = 268.69 \text{ ft}$$

The offset distance is calculated using Eq. 6-12. In this calculation χ_c becomes χ.

$$d = \frac{\chi^2(G_1 - G_2)}{2L}$$
$$= \frac{(97.78)^2(-0.05 - 0.022)}{2 \times 320 \text{ ft}} \qquad (6\text{-}12)$$
$$= 1.08 \text{ ft}$$

The vertical offset distance must be added (on a sag curve) to the elevation on the tangent at the station of the critical point.

$$268.69 \text{ ft} + 1.08 \text{ ft} = 269.77 \text{ ft}$$

The catch basin should be located at sta 25+62.22 where the elevation is

269.77. The elevation at the top of the grate (TG) of the catch basin will be somewhat lower because of the cross slope of the street.

Calculations for the profile should be recorded in an orderly manner. A Profile Calculations form is given as Fig. 6-11. An example of the completed form is shown in Fig. 6-12. Notice that a profile with a station equation is illustrated.

PROFILE CALCULATIONS

Station	Slope	VC	Elev. on tangent	Vert. offset	Elev.	Station	Slope	VC	Elev. on tangent	Vert. offset	Elev.

Fig. 6-11   Profile calculations form.

PROFILE CALCULATIONS

Station	Slope	VC	Elev. on tangent	Vert. offset	Elev.	Station	Slope	VC	Elev. on tangent	Vert. offset	Elev.
49 + 00			223.03		223.03						
50 + 00	S = −0.034				219.63						
51 + 00					216.23						
51 + 25.80	New ₵	=			215.35						
51 + 73.63	EX ₵										
52 + 00					214.45						
53 + 00					211.05						
53 + 50		BVC	209.35	0	209.35						
54 + 00		200-ft VC	207.65	0.09	207.56						
54 + 50	PI		205.95	0.35	205.60						
55 + 00			203.55	0.09	203.46						
55 + 50	−0.048	EVC	201.15	0	201.15						
56 + 00					198.75						
57 + 00					196.35						

Fig. 6-12 Profile calculations form filled out.

106

Grades

Consideration must be given to limiting the steepness of slopes used for streets and roads. The approving agency will have minimum and maximum grade limits. The maximum slope to be used for long distances of highway may be as low as 6 percent. This grade is chosen to provide a slope at which a heavily laden truck can be expected to climb safely. The safety of descending a grade with a heavy load is just as important.

City streets may be designed with grades as steep as 15 percent for short distances. For a private road, 20 percent may be used if allowed by local agencies. Here, access for emergency vehicles, such as fire trucks, is a consideration.

Where streets have slopes of 10 percent or greater, it may be wise to limit parking. The force of gravity becomes a factor in handling car doors where the slope of the parking area is steep. An unwieldy door can be a hazard for small adults or for children.

When a road is in open country and can be built above the surrounding land, the road can drain laterally and the longitudinal grade can actually be level. When streets are designed in subdivisions, they may be used to channel and control storm water and must be designed with longitudinal grades sufficient to allow drainage.

A slope of 0.003 is an absolute minimum. Successful construction of a slope that flat is questionable and bird baths (small puddles) are likely to develop. Use a steeper slope whenever possible. The approving agency will dictate the minimum allowable slope.

Drainage Release Points

An important consideration in designing street profiles is provision for drainage release points. If the storm water inlets do not function for some reason, or if a storm is greater than design capacity, the storm water will rise until it reaches an elevation at which it can flow from one drainage basin to the next basin. That elevation and its horizontal location is the *drainage release point*. An acceptable depth of flooding is determined, and release points no higher above the low point in the drainage basin than the acceptable depth of flooding must be provided (Fig. 6-13).

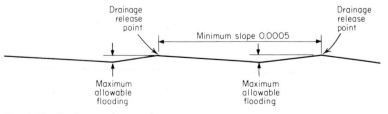

Fig. 6-13 Drainage release point.

When a subdivision is to be designed in a very flat area, the natural fall of the land may not allow for a 0.003 slope. Here, slopes must be manufactured with a zigzag design for the profiles. The profile should be designed with a grade of negative 0.003 for a distance and then with a grade of positive 0.003. The distance for the positive slope must be shorter than the distance for the negative slope so that there will be a negative slope between successive high points (Fig. 6-13) of no less than 0.0005. At street intersections care should be taken to determine the drainage release point.

At street intersections the intersecting curbs are connected with short radius (20 to 40 ft) curves. These are called *curb returns*. The radius to use will be dictated by the approving agency. These connections need to be examined for drainage. There should be enough fall from one end of return (ER) to the other to provide a slope of 0.004 around the curb return. If this slope cannot be provided, one of the street profiles may have to be redesigned. An alternative is to increase the cross slope of one of the streets at the end of the curb return enough to provide a clear low point of drainage. The low point should be at an ER. Placing catch basins within curb returns should be avoided.

Abrupt changes in the profile of the curbs are undesirable. Where the difference in street grades exceeds 5 percent or the elevations at the ends of the returns differ by more than 0.5 ft, profiles of the curb returns should be drawn and curves used where necessary for smooth transitions. Curves can be calculated or simply drawn into the profile. Elevations at the midpoint of the return and at quarter points can then be measured from the profile and marked on the plan view (Fig. 6-14).

Sight Distances

The distance that a driver can see ahead on the road is called the *sight distance*. The distance along the road that a driver must be able to see ahead to safely pass a car going at a particular speed is called the *passing sight distance*.

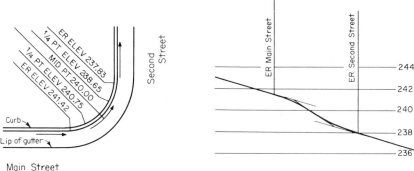

Fig. 6-14 Curb return.

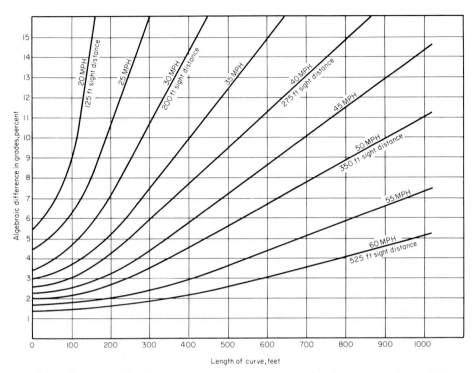

Fig. 6-15 Stopping sight distances on crest vertical curves; based on height of eye, 3.75 ft, height of object, 0.5 ft.

The distance it takes a driver, traveling at a particular speed, to stop his or her car after seeing an object in the road is called the *stopping sight distance.*

Streets and roads are designed to allow traffic to travel at particular speeds. The speed of traffic determines the necessary stopping and passing sight distances. The desirable stopping or passing sight distances dictate the lengths of vertical curves necessary to provide safe driving through grade changes.

A chart is provided in Fig. 6-15 for selecting the appropriate stopping sight distance on a crest vertical curve. A chart providing curve lengths for stopping sight distances on a sag curve is provided in Fig. 6-16.

Example 6-6

Determine the length to use for a vertical curve when the entering slope is plus 1 percent and the exiting slope is plus 6 percent. The design speed is 50 mph.

Solution

1. The curve is a sag curve because the slope goes from a positive slope to a steeper positive slope.

2. The algebraic difference in grades is

$$(+6) - (+1) = 5 \text{ percent}$$

3. Enter the chart for stopping sight distance in a sag curve at 5 percent on the left side. Follow the 5 percent line to its intersection with the 50-mph line. The length of the curve to use is 380 ft, as read directly below the intersection on the length-of-curve scale.

CROSS-SECTIONAL DESIGN

The approving agency usually dictates the geometric and structural cross sections to be used for streets that will eventually be dedicated to public use and will become their responsibility to maintain.

Geometric Cross Sections

Geometric cross sections are used in the planning stages of projects. The widths and dimensions of the various elements of the street are shown. The width of the right-of-way is based on the expected traffic volumes. A standard width for traffic lanes is 12 ft. Also shown on the geometric cross section may be widths

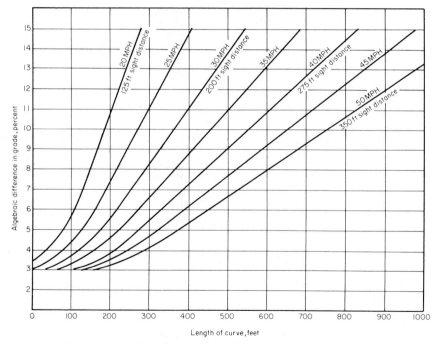

Fig. 6-16 Stopping sight distances on sag vertical curves.

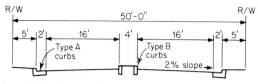

Fig. 6-17   Geometric cross section.

of shoulders, bicycle lanes, medians, curbs and gutters, sidewalks, and planting strips (see Fig. 6-17). Cross slopes on paved sections may be shown. Cross slopes range from 2 to 4 percent on traveled ways and up to 5 percent on shoulders.

Structural Cross Sections

The types of materials to be used for the construction of streets, their thicknesses, and other specific information are shown on the structural cross section (see Fig. 6-18). The choice of material is based on the expected traffic loads and the characteristics of the supporting soil. The types of curb required and the type of sidewalk will be shown. The geometric dimensions are also included.

Curbs and Gutters

There are six basic types of curbs (Fig. 6-19).

1. *Curb with gutter.* Typically the gutter is 1.5 to 2.0 ft wide (Fig. 6-19*a*).
2. *Vertical curb with spill gutter.* The gutter is sloped away from the curb and is used along medians and in other places where the street is sloped away from the curb (Fig. 6-19*b*).
3. *Rolled curb.* When the street improvements are built before improvements to the lots are planned, a rolled curb may be used. The advantage of the rolled curb is that it can be driven over. This way, when improvements to the lots are made, the driveway can be located anywhere along the property without requiring that the curb be removed and replaced by a driveway cut. The disadvantage of using rolled curbs is that driving over them can

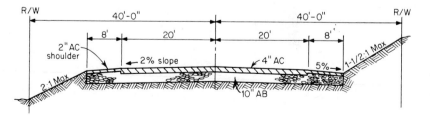

Fig. 6-18   Structural cross section.

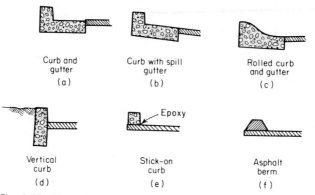

Fig. 6-19 Typical curbs.

adversely affect the front-end alignment on cars, and they provide less protection for pedestrians (Fig. 6-19c).

4. *Vertical curb.* This curb extends below as well as above the pavement. It is used around medians, islands, and planters (Fig. 6-19d).

5. *Stick-on (extruded) curb.* This curb is used extensively in parking lot design. This concrete curb is attached to the paved surface with epoxy (Fig. 6-19e).

6. *Asphalt berm or dike.* This AC curb is usually used in rural areas to direct drainage (Fig. 6-19f).

Superelevations

On straight sections of streets and roads the cross slope ranges from 1 to 4 percent away from the centerline so that the water will drain off. This is called the *crown.* When the horizontal alignment of roads is curved and speeds greater

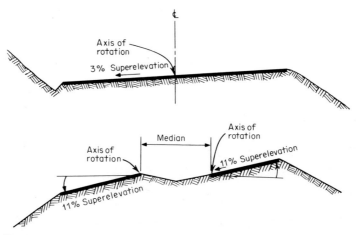

Fig. 6-20 Superelevations.

than 30 mph are expected, centrifugal force becomes a factor affecting a safe, comfortable ride.

To overcome centrifugal force, the cross slope is tilted up on the outside of the curve. This tilting is called *superelevation* (Fig. 6-20). Design of superelevations is within the realm of highway design and is beyond the scope of this book.

On private driveways built on the side of a hill, the road may be sloped toward the cut side to facilitate drainage regardless of curves, because, if the street drainage is allowed to flow over the embankment, erosion will occur. Of course, whether this can be done safely depends on the expected traffic speed, which in turn is based on the length and steepness of the driveway slope.

MEETING EXISTING STREETS

Often it will be necessary to meet a half street and complete it to full width or to widen an already existing street and construct curbs. When this is the assignment, an examination of the existing street is essential. Determine the width and condition of the existing pavement. Should it be removed and replaced? Will an asphalt overlay be needed? If it is to remain, should the new section overlay the old one to conform, or should a sharp edge be cut and a butt joint made? Is there a shoulder or temporary paving that will have to be removed? The approving agency may provide the answers to these questions, but you should satisfy yourself that they are the right choices.

When the assignment is to meet an existing edge of pavement longitudinally, the existing edge of pavement must be plotted at an exaggerated scale, such as 1 in = 20 ft horizontally, 1 in = 2 ft vertically. Use of the exaggerated scale makes any deviation from a smooth profile apparent. Profiles should also be plotted where the new edge of the pavement will fall if the cross slope is 1 and if the cross slope is 4 percent. If the new edge of the pavement is to be 25 ft from the old one, the new profiles will be below the existing profile at 0.25 ft (0.01 × 25 ft) and 1.0 ft (0.04 × 25 ft). An edge of the pavement within the area between these profiles will provide a satisfactory cross slope (Fig. 6-21). If

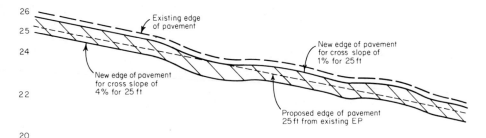

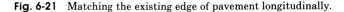

Fig. 6-21 Matching the existing edge of pavement longitudinally.

the existing edge of the pavement is very uneven, dips must be filled in with asphalt, and humps must be scraped off to provide a smooth ride.

The design of a new curb should be handled in a similar manner. Calculate the elevation difference between the joint and the new curb for a 1 percent cross slope and a 4 percent cross slope. Draw the profiles of these elevations. Design the profile of the new curb to fall between the two profiles. Make the cross slope of the new section match the cross slope of the existing section as much as possible. Cross sections are helpful in coordinating cross slopes and profiles. If there is to be an asphalt overlay of the existing section, the depth must be added to the existing profiles when calculating the new profiles.

Be alert to existing facilities. At the location of overlays, manhole rims and covers will have to be adjusted to the grade. If sidewalks and curbs are being added or relocated, underground power lines, transformers, or junction boxes may be affected.

PARKING LOTS

The plan view layout of parking lots is usually designed by architects or planners and is based on a requirement for certain width driving lanes and a certain number of parking spaces per square foot of commercial or industrial space.

The engineer's task is to design the lot so that water will drain away from the buildings without hampering the use of the parking lot. The amount and direction of fall across the lot will influence, if not dictate, how the lot should be drained. Most jurisdictions will not allow parking lots to drain over the sidewalk. This precludes draining the lot through the driveway as well.

The elevations and conditions at the boundary influences how to approach the design. Determine if it will be necessary to provide ditches or retaining walls along the property lines.

Parking lots can be sloped to drain toward curbs and gutters at the sides or toward area drains in the driving lanes. There may be an increased risk of the storm water inlet being blocked by a tire or an accumulation of trash where the drainage is at the side, but there are significant advantages. If the curb and gutter at the side is used, the drainage in the longitudinal direction can be at a slope of 0.004. This flat slope will allow a greater distance between inlets resulting in fewer inlets. Also less zigzagging of the profile will be required. A concrete curb and gutter is strong and will provide enduring drainage control.

A nearly flat slope can also be accomplished with a valley gutter (Fig. 6-22) down the center of the traveled way. It is more expensive to build a valley gutter down the driveway and a curb at the edge of the parking than to simply build a curb and gutter at the edge. Valley gutters in driveways are more subject to failure as well. However, valley gutters are clearly indicated in apartment and

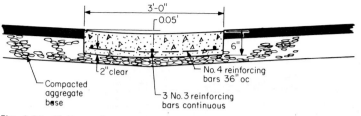

Fig. 6-22 Valley gutter.

similar projects where garages are on either side of the driveway and there is little design flexibility.

A popular way to drain parking lots is to divide them into sections and drain toward the center of each section. If drainage reaches of 50 ft or less are used, a minimum slope of 1 percent can be used. Slopes must be set in critical directions. The critical direction is often between the inlet and the farthest corner of the area draining into it. The slopes must then be checked between the inlet and all other high and low points in the area of drainage (Fig. 6-23) to verify that the minimum and maximum slope criteria are not exceeded. This method works well, and the slope is not noticeable to those using the lot. If drainage reaches longer than 50 ft are chosen to minimize the number of inlets required, the minimum slope should be 2 percent. When 2 percent is used as the minimum slope in the longitudinal direction, the slopes in the short direction are much steeper, and a bowl effect results. Architects and others concerned with

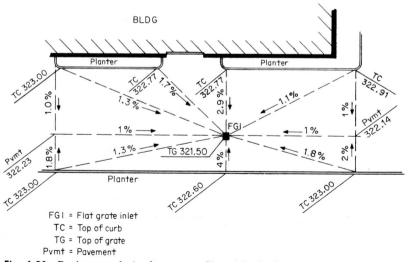

FGI = Flat grate inlet
TC = Top of curb
TG = Top of grate
Pvmt = Pavement

Fig. 6-23 Paving area drained to center. Slopes checked.

Fig. 6-24 Car on 7 percent cross slope.

aesthetics often object to this bowl-like appearance. A maximum slope of 4 percent should be used in parking areas (Fig. 6-24).

The drainage release point needs to be examined for parking lots. The lots should be designed so that if all the inlets did not function, the storm water would flood to no more than 1 ft deep before spilling over into the adjacent area.

REFERENCES

The American Association of State Highway and Transportation Officials: Various publications, Washington, D.C.

State of California, Department of Transportation Chief, Office of Planning and Design: *Highway Design Manual,* Sacramento, CA.

Chapter Seven

Sanitary Sewers

Collection and treatment of sewage is the most critical element in the development of a site. Without a plan for safe disposal of sewage, a site cannot be developed.

In most cases, a sewer system can be accommodated simply by installing a gravity-flow sewer network and connecting it to an existing public sewer system. When a site is too low to allow gravity flow or when there are no public systems in the area, the problem becomes more complicated.

The design of a gravity-flow sewer network will be described in this chapter. The use of force mains and septic systems will be discussed briefly.

SOURCES AND QUANTITIES

Determining the quantity of sewage is of primary importance when designing a sewerage network. The sanitary sewer district or agency which will treat and dispose of the effluent must be consulted. The agency should have a master sanitary sewer plan based on expected future growth as well as on existing needs. The quantity of sewage per unit and the size of conduits to use within your project may be dictated by the agency. The master plan may require installation of a conduit larger than necessary to accommodate your project alone. When this is the case, compensation may be paid or credited to the builder for the extent of upgrading the sewer. If the responsible jurisdiction does not dictate quantity, you must determine what quantity to use to design the system.

Sewage Production

The use of the site, whether residential, commercial, or industrial, influences expected flows. Sewage flows are also directly related to water consumption. "In general . . . about 60 to 80 percent of the per capita consumption of water will become sewage."[1] For this reason, begin by looking at water consumption when other sources of flow rate information are not available.

As illustrated in Table 7-1, consumption rates vary considerably from area to area. Notice in the table that water consumption ranges from 50 gpd/cap (50 gallons per day per capita) in Little Rock, Arkansas, to 410 gpd/cap in Las Vegas, Nevada. In Las Vegas, 51 percent of the water consumed reached the sewer system. In Little Rock, 100 percent of the water consumed reached the sanitary sewer. The differences in amounts of water used are affected by such things as climate, distribution of land uses, cost of water, availability of non-public sources of water, and cultural attitudes.

Table 9-1 lists water consumption based on production volumes for various industries. Table 9-2 lists estimated water consumption for various types of nonindustrial establishments. To estimate sewage flow rates on a particular project, you must determine the percentage of water consumed that does not reach the sanitary sewer lines. If the project is a park, a low percentage of the water consumed will reach the sanitary sewer system. On the other hand, in a meat processing plant, a high percentage of the water consumed will reach the sanitary system. The best figures to use in the case of an industrial site are ones supplied by the client. Accurate water consumption figures and an estimate of the percentage reaching the sanitary system should be available.

The Fixture-Unit Method

The use of the fixture-unit method for estimating flows from hotels, apartments, hospitals, schools, and office buildings is often indicated. The United States of America Standards Institute National Plumbing Code, USASI A40.8-1955, defines a fixture unit as

a quantity in terms of which the load producing effects on the plumbing system of different kinds of plumbing fixtures are expressed on some arbitrarily chosen scale.

The quantity is approximately 1 cfm (7.5 gpm). Table 7-2 lists some examples of fixture-unit values for various facilities.

The Peaking Factor

The sewer flow rate varies during the day. Because of this fluctuation, the sewer sizes are not designed for the average flow, but are designed for peak flows. The *peak flow* is the highest instantaneous rate of flow occurring during the day.

[1]Metcalf & Eddy, Inc.: *Wastewater Engineering,* McGraw-Hill Book Co., New York, 1972, p. 33.

TABLE 7-1 Some Typical Design Flows*

City	Year and Source of Data	Average Rate of Water Consumption, gpd/cap	Population Served, 1000s	Average Sewage Flow, gpd/cap	Sewer Design Basis, gpd/cap	Remarks
Baltimore, MD	—	160	1300	100	135 × factor	Factor 4 to 2.
Berkeley, CA	—	76	113	60	92	
Boston, MA	—	145	801	140	150	Flowing half full.
Cleveland, OH	1946 (6)	—	—	100	—	
Cranston, RI	1943 (6)	—	—	119	167	
Des Moines, IA	1949 (6)	—	—	100	200	
Grand Rapids, MI	—	178	200	190	200	
Greenville County, SC	1959	110	200	150	300	Service area includes city of Greenville. Sewers 24 in and less designed to flow ⅔ full at 300 gpd/cap; sewers larger than 24 in designed to have 1-ft freeboard.
Hagerstown, MD	—	100	38	100	250	
Jefferson County, AL	—	102	500	100	300	
Johnson County, KS Mission Township main sewer dist.	1958	70	70	60	1350	Most houses have basements with exterior foundation drains.
Indian Creek main sewer dist.	1958	70	30	60	675	Most houses have basements with interior foundation drains.
Kansas City, MO	1958	—	500	60	675	For trunks and interceptors.
					1350	For laterals and submains. Many houses have basements and exterior foundation drains.
Lancaster County, NB	1962	167	148	92	400	Serves city of Lincoln.
Las Vegas, NV	—	410	45	209	250	

119

TABLE 7-1 Some Typical Design Flows* (continued)

City	Year and Source of Data	Average Rate of Water Consumption, gpd/cap	Population Served, 1000s	Average Sewage Flow, gpd/cap	Sewer Design Basis, gpd/cap	Remarks
Lincoln, NB lateral dists.	1964			60		For lateral sewers max flow by formula: peak flow = 5 × avg flow ÷ (pop in 1000s)$^{0.2}$.
Little Rock, AR	—	50	100	50	100	
Los Angeles, CA	1965	185	2710	85	†	
Los Angeles County sanitation dist.	1964	200	3500	70‡	—	
Greater Peoria, IL	1960	90	150	75	800 / 8500	Based on 12 persons per acre for lateral and trunk sewers, respectively.
Madison, WI	1937 (6)	—	—	—	300	Maximum hourly rate.
Milwaukee, WI	1945 (6)	—	—	125	—	All in 12 h 250 gpd/cap rate.
Memphis, TN	—	125	450	100	100	
Orlando, FL	—	150	75	70	190	
Painesville, OH	1947 (6)	—	—	125	600	Includes infiltration and roof water.
Rapid City, SD	—	122	40	121	125	New York State Board of Health Standard.
Rochester, NY	1946 (6)	—	—	—	250	
Santa Monica, CA	—	137	75	92	92	
Shreveport, LA	1961	125	165	—	—	Sewer design 150 gpd/cap plus 600 gpd/acre infiltration. Sewers 24 in and less designed to flow ½ full; sewers larger than 24 in designed to have 1-ft freeboard.
St. Joseph, MO	1960	—	85	125	450 / 350	Main sewers. Interceptors.

Springfield, MA	1949 (5)	—	—	—	200	150 gpd/cap was used on a special project.
Toledo, OH	1946 (5)	—	—	—	160	
Washington, DC suburban sanitary dist.	1946 (5)	—	—	100	2 to 3.3 × avg	
Wyoming, MI	1960	150	50	82§	400	

*Taken from the American Society of Civil Engineers and the Water Pollution Federation: *Design and Construction of Sanitary and Storm Sewers*, New York, 1979.

†The 85 gpd residential multiplied by peak factor. See Fig. 7-6.

‡Domestic flow only, ranges from 50 to 90 gpd/cap depending on cost of water, type of residence, etc. Domestic plus industrial averages 90 gpd.

§Calculated actual domestic sewage flow not including infiltration or industrial flow.

NOTE: Gal × 3.785 = 1; gpd/acre × 0.00935 = m³/day/ha; ft × 0.3 = m; in × 2.54 = cm.

Figure 7-1 is a graph of an hourly variation of sewage flow. The peak flow occurs between 1 and 2 p.m. on the graph.

A *peaking factor* is a multiplier applied to the average flow to yield the largest amount of flow expected. For example, if the average flow expected throughout the day is 400 gpd/cap (16.6 gph/cap), the peak flow may occur between 1 and 2 p.m. and be 800 gpd/cap (33.2 gph/cap). Here the peaking factor is 2. The peak flow is two times as large as the average flow. The conduits must be

TABLE 7-2 Fixture Units per Fixture or Group*

Fixture Type	Fixture-Unit Value as Load Factors
1 bathroom group consisting of tank-operated water closet, lavatory, and bathtub or shower stall	6
Bathtub (with or without overhead shower)†	2
Bidet	3
Combination sink-and-tray	3
Combination sink-and-tray with food disposal unit	4
Dental unit or cuspidor	1
Dental lavatory	1
Drinking fountain	½
Dishwasher, domestic	2
Floor drains	1
Kitchen sink, domestic	2
Kitchen sink, domestic, with food waste grinder	3
Lavatory	1
Lavatory	2
Lavatory, barber, beauty parlor	2
Lavatory, surgeon's	2
Laundry tray (1 or 2 compartments)	2
Shower stall, domestic	2
Showers (group) per head	3
Sinks	
Surgeon's	3
Flushing rim (with valve)	8
Service (trap standard)	3
Service (P trap)	2
Pot, scullery, etc.	4
Urinal, pedestal, syphon jet, blowout	8
Urinal, wall lip	4
Urinal stall, washout	4
Urinal trough (each 2-ft section)	2
Wash sink (circular or multiple) each set of faucets	2
Water closet, tank-operated	4
Water closet, valve-operated	8

*From United States of America Standards Institute National Plumbing Code, USASI A40.8-1955.

†A shower head over a bathtub does not increase the fixture value.

NOTE: For a continuous or semicontinuous flow into a drainage system, such as from a pump, pump ejector, air-conditioning equipment, or similar device, two fixture units shall be allowed for each gpm of flow.

designed to accommodate the peak flow if the system is to function adequately. Depending upon the number of sources contributing to the sewer, the peaking factor will vary between 1.3 and 2. The agency may dictate a peaking factor.

Infiltration

On large projects, infiltration of groundwater into the sanitary sewers may be a factor in sizing the pipe. Check with the governing agency as to what infiltration rate should be added. Infiltration rates used are generally in the range of 250 to 500 gpd per inch of diameter per mile of pipe.

HYDRAULICS

The science of the mechanics of fluids at rest and in motion is called *hydraulics*. The study of hydraulics is an intellectual and complicated endeavor. Fortunately, however, knowledge of two hydraulics equations and the ability to use a hydraulics calculator are usually all that is needed to design the simple gravity-flow sewer networks found in most land development projects. The two hydraulics equations, the continuity equation and Manning's equation, will be discussed in this section.

The Continuity Equation

The most basic hydraulics equation is the continuity equation. Stated simply it says the quantity (Q) of fluid passing a particular point is the result of its velocity (V) and the cross-sectional area (A) of the flow. The continuity equation is

$$Q = VA \qquad\qquad (7\text{-}1)$$

where Q = quantity, cfs
        V = velocity, fps
        A = cross-sectional area, ft^2

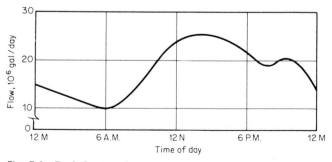

Fig. 7-1 Peak flow graph.

The quantity is often referred to as the flow rate or capacity. This equation is used to determine the size and slope of the pipe used in the sewer network.

The slope of the pipe is a function of the velocity and will be discussed under Manning's equation. The size of the pipe is designated by its diameter. Using the required area, the diameter of the conduit can be calculated using the equation for the area of a circle.

$$A = \pi r^2 \qquad (7\text{-}2)$$
$$= \pi \left(\frac{D}{2}\right)^2$$

Algebraic manipulation yields the value for the diameter (D) as a function of the area.

$$D = \left(\frac{4A}{\pi}\right)^{1/2} \qquad (7\text{-}3)$$

To determine the diameter, a value for the required area is needed. The continuity equation can be manipulated algebraically to yield the area of the pipe required for a particular velocity.

$$A_R = \frac{Q}{V} \qquad (7\text{-}4)$$

where A_R = cross-sectional area required, ft^2
  Q = quantity, cfs
  V = velocity, fps

The maximum capacity of a pipe is reached when the pipe is filled to $0.8D$. Beyond this point, the increase in friction reduces the velocity, and thus the capacity. A conservative approximation can be made by assuming that the pipe is flowing full.

Example 7-1

Determine the size of pipe needed to transport 7.5 cfs of sewage at a minimum velocity of 2 fps. Assume the pipe is flowing full.

Solution

The quantity (Q) is 7.5 cfs. The velocity (V) is 2 fps.

1. Using Eq. 7-4

$$A_R = \frac{Q}{V} \qquad (7\text{-}4)$$
$$= \frac{7.5 \text{ cfs}}{2 \text{ fps}}$$
$$= 3.75 \text{ ft}^2$$

2. Using Eq. 7-3

$$D = \left(\frac{4A}{\pi}\right)^{1/2}$$
$$= \left(\frac{4 \times 3.75 \text{ ft}^2}{3.14}\right)^{1/2}$$
$$= 2.19 \text{ ft}$$

Converting to inches

$$2.19 \text{ ft} \times \frac{12 \text{ in}}{\text{ft}} = 26.22 \text{ in}$$

Pipes are manufactured with various standard diameters. Table 7-3 shows commonly available sizes. When the required diameter for a particular flow falls between standard sizes, the larger size must be used. Commonly, there are 24-in-diameter pipes and 27-in-diameter pipes available. Since 26.22 in falls between the two, use the larger (27-in) pipe.

The problem with this approach to selecting pipe sizes is that it does not provide information about what slope will be required nor does it provide the flexibility of using a velocity greater than minimum. The continuity equation shows that a greater velocity will allow use of a smaller diameter pipe while transporting the same quantity of flow. Manning's equation provides needed relationships about velocity and slope.

Manning's Equation

The relationships among the various factors affecting the velocity of flow in pipes are expressed in Manning's equation. Though there are other formulas relating the factors of flow, Manning's is the most commonly used. Manning's equation is given in Eq. 7-5.

$$V = \frac{1.49}{n} R_H^{2/3} S^{1/2} \tag{7-5}$$

where V = velocity, fps
n = coefficient of roughness
R_H = hydraulic radius, ft
S = slope, feet per foot

The value of 1.49 accounts for dimensional differences.[2] The n is referred to as Manning's n and is a friction factor for the roughness of the pipe. The value of n to use may be dictated by the responsible jurisdiction. Otherwise, 0.013 can be used for concrete or vitrified clay pipe (VCP). Values of n for other materials are given in Table 8-2. The smoother the conduit, the smaller the

[2]When metric dimensions are used, this factor is 1.000.

TABLE 7-3 Pipe Sizes

Concrete Pipe Size						
Pipe Size Inside Diameter, in	Shell Thickness		Invert to Top of Pipe, ft	Outside Diameter, ft	Trench Width, ft	Pipe Size Inside Diameter, in
	in	ft				
8	1½	0.12	0.79	0.91	2.00	8
10	1⅜	0.11	0.94	1.05	2.05	10
12	1⅝	0.14	1.14	1.28	2.28	12
15	2¾	0.23	1.48	1.71	2.71	15
18	2½	0.21	1.71	1.92	2.92	18
21	2⅝	0.22	1.97	2.19	3.19	21
24	3⅝	0.30	2.30	2.60	3.60	24
27	3½	0.29	2.54	2.82	4.15	27
30	3¾	0.31	2.81	3.12	4.45	30
33	3¾	0.31	3.06	3.37	4.70	33
36	4⅝	0.39	3.39	3.78	5.11	36
42	5	0.42	3.92	4.34	5.67	42
48	5½	.46	4.46	4.92	6.25	48
54	6	0.50	5.00	5.50	6.83	54
60	6½	0.54	5.54	6.08	7.41	60
66	7	0.58	6.08	6.66	7.99	66
72	7½	.63	6.63	7.26	8.59	72
78	8	0.67	7.16	7.83	9.16	78
84	8½	0.71	7.71	8.42	9.75	84
90	8½	0.71	8.21	8.92	10.25	90
96	9	0.75	8.75	9.50	10.83	96

Vitrified Clay Pipe Size							
Pipe Size, in	Thickness		Invert to Top of Pipe, ft	Outside Barrel Diameter, ft	Outside Bell Diameter, ft	Invert to Top of Bell, ft	Trench Width, ft	Pipe Size, in
	in	ft						
4	⅝	0.05	0.38	0.44	0.59	0.43	2.00	4
6	¹¹⁄₁₆	0.055	0.555	0.61	0.81	0.66	2.00	6
8	⅞	0.07	0.74	0.81	1.02	0.845	2.00	8
10	1	0.08	0.91	1.00	1.22	1.025	2.00	10
12	1³⁄₁₆	0.095	1.095	1.19	1.45	1.225	2.19	12
15	1½	0.12	1.37	1.49	1.77	1.51	2.49	15
18	1⅞	0.155	1.655	1.81	2.09	1.795	2.81	18
21	2¼	0.19	1.94	2.13	2.42	2.085	3.13	21
24	2½	0.21	2.21	2.42	2.78	2.40	3.42	24
27	2¾	0.23	2.48	2.71	3.10	2.665	4.04	27
30	3	0.25	2.75	3.00	3.46	2.955	4.33	30
33	3¼	0.27	3.02	3.29	3.77	3.23	4.62	33
36	3½	0.29	3.29	3.58	4.07	3.54	4.91	36
39	3²⁵⁄₃₂	0.315	3.565	3.88	4.45	3.815	4.21	39

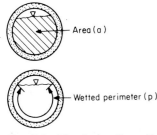

Fig. 7-2 The hydraulic radius (R_H) = area/wetted perimeter.

value of n. From Manning's equation (Eq. 7-5), we see that the smoother the pipe to be used, the greater the velocity that is produced.

R_H in the equation is the hydraulic radius. It accounts for the effect of friction on the flow. The value of R_H is expressed in Eq. 7-6.

$$R_H = \frac{a}{p} \tag{7-6}$$

where R_H = hydraulic radius
$\qquad a$ = cross-sectional area of the flow
$\qquad p$ = wetted perimeter

The wetted perimeter (Fig. 7-2) is the length measured on the cross section that will be wet when the pipe is flowing at the designated capacity.

Using the continuity equation and Manning's equation, the quantity can be calculated. For design purposes on simple projects, pipes can be assumed to be flowing full,[3] and a value for the slope is taken from the designed profile.

Example 7-2

Find the capacity of a 12-in conduit flowing full and installed at a slope of 0.005. Use 0.013 as Manning's n.

Solution

We are given S = 0.005, D = 12 in, and n = 0.013. The formula for flow rate is $Q = AV$ (Eq. 7-1).

1. Calculate the cross-sectional area of the 12-in-diameter pipe.

$$A = \frac{\pi D^2}{4}$$

[3]The maximum capacity is reached when the pipe is filled to $0.8D$. Beyond this point the increase in friction due to the increase in wetted perimeter slows the velocity. Assuming that the pipe is flowing full yields a conservative capacity.

$$= \frac{3.14(1 \text{ ft})^2}{4}$$
$$= 0.78 \text{ ft}^2$$

2. Calculate velocity (V) using Manning's equation.

$$V = \frac{1.49}{n} R_H^{2/3} S^{1/2} \qquad (7\text{-}5)$$

We have been given n and S. We must calculate R_H.

$$R_H = \frac{a}{p} \qquad (7\text{-}6)$$

As the pipe is flowing full, the area equals the area of the pipe; the wetted perimeter equals the circumference.

$$R_H = \frac{\pi D^2 / 4}{\pi D}$$

All the factors cancel except $D/4$.

$$R_H = \frac{D}{4} \qquad (7\text{-}7)$$
$$R_H = 0.25 \text{ ft}$$

Inserting values into Manning's equation we get

$$V = \frac{1.49}{0.013} (0.25)^{2/3}(0.005)^{1/2}$$
$$= \frac{1.49}{0.013} (0.397)(0.071)$$
$$= 3.23 \text{ fps}$$

Now all the factors are available. The flow rate can be calculated using Eq. 7-1.

$$Q = AV$$
$$= 0.78 \text{ ft}^2 \times 3.23 \text{ fps} \qquad (7\text{-}1)$$
$$= 2.52 \text{ cfs}$$

THE SEWER NETWORK

The sanitary sewer network is usually the first of the utilities to be designed. It is desirable, if not necessary, that the system be a gravity-flow system. That is, the sewage will be transported from the site to the treatment facility by the force of gravity—no pumping will be necessary. Ordinarily the only available outfalls are previously existing sanitary sewer networks, so there is little flexibility available to the designer.

The storm sewer network will also be a gravity-flow system, but there are usually more outfalls available, and alternatives other than connections to existing networks can be used. Another factor is the depth of the sanitary sewer.

There is less flexibility in the vertical location for sanitary sewers than for storm sewers.

Design of the sewer network requires accommodation of many factors: the physical conditions of the existing and proposed site, the physical laws of hydraulics, construction technology, cost considerations, and criteria established by the sanitation agency.

The agency may dictate criteria for horizontal and depth locations, velocity of flow, and/or minimum and maximum slopes, minimum pipe sizes, types, and classes. The agency should have a master sanitary sewer plan that will accommodate sanitary sewer needs on an areawide basis for the future as well as for the present.

Laterals

Design of plumbing within buildings is ordinarily the responsibility of the architect or mechanical engineer. A connection from the building to the sewer mains should be provided by the civil engineer designing the site improvements. This connection is called a *lateral.* The architect should be consulted as to what is the best horizontal location for the lateral. When the job is to provide the sewer main in the streets for residential lots, the laterals may extend only from the main to the property line.

A sewer cleanout (Fig. 7-3) may be required at the property line. When the cleanout is to be located in a street or driveway, a frame and cover capable of withstanding traffic must be provided. It is desirable to locate the cleanouts in landscaped areas rather than in driveways. The additional expense of providing

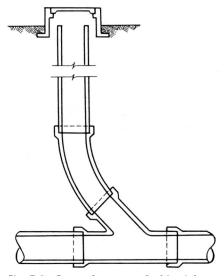

Fig. 7-3 Sewer cleanout or flushing inlet.

cleanout frames and covers for traffic areas is significant on projects where multiple buildings will be served. When the location and orientation of the buildings and/or driveways on residential lots have not been determined, the center of the lot is usually a good choice for the lateral. This way the driveway should fall on one or the other side of the lateral, and the cleanout will be in the lawn or landscaped area.

Backflow prevention or check valves should be provided in laterals where the next upstream manhole on the sewer main is at an elevation above the floor of the building being served (Fig. 7-4). The reason for this is that if the sewer main downstream of the lateral fails to function, the sewage will back up and overflow at the first available opening. If the top of the next upstream manhole is below the plumbing facilities within the house, the overflow will occur at the manhole. Any openings in the system (bathtubs, toilets, and sinks) with openings below the top of the next upstream manhole will provide a relief opening for overflow unless protected by a check valve. The check valve should be located where the building plumbing discharges into the lateral.

The lateral should be connected to the main with a wye and a bend. The sewer main must be deep enough to allow the lateral to reach from below the building foundation[4] to the sewer main with a slope of at least 2 percent and to allow for the wye and bend (Fig. 7-5).

Horizontal Location of the Main

A project master plan should be prepared for sites that may have utilities crossing. The scale should be selected to show the entire site and any off-site connections. A copy of the grading plan or tentative map should serve well as a base map. The project master plan is a working drawing. All existing utilities

[4]Sewer laterals can be built through structures, but it is an expense that should be avoided.

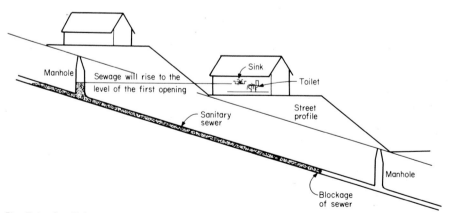

Fig. 7-4 Condition requiring a backflow prevention device.

must be shown and their locations dimensioned. All potential outfalls should be identified. A *sanitary sewer outfall* is an existing main or manhole into which the sewer can be discharged.

The invert elevations of the outfalls should be labeled on the master plan. The *invert elevation* is the elevation at the inside bottom of the pipe. Using this information and approximate slopes for the pipes, locations of potential crossing conflicts can be identified and alternate solutions worked out before much work is done.

The utility for which there is the least design flexibility available should be designed first. This is usually the sanitary sewer. The approving jurisdiction may require that the sewer have a particular location, such as 5 ft north or east of the centerline. If the horizontal location is not dictated, locate the sanitary main where it will make the least number of crossings with existing utilities and where the length of the laterals will be minimized.

Manholes must be provided where sewer mains connect and where there is a change of direction in the main. Some jurisdictions allow horizontal curves for directional changes, some do not. Whatever criteria are dictated must be adhered to. Curves may be allowed if manholes are provided at the beginning and/or end of the curves or at intermediate locations within the curves. Where curves are used, relevant curve data should be calculated and shown on the plans. Calculation of curve data is described in Chap. 6. Minimum curve radii or allowable deflections are provided by pipe manufacturers.

Designing the Profile

When a tentative horizontal layout is complete, a profile for the conduit can be designed. On profile paper, plot to scale the existing and proposed groundline. Plot all crossings of existing utilities and other underground obstacles. Elevations at the top or bottom of crossing utilities should be calculated and marked on the plan.

Begin the design of the conduit profile at the outfall, and project the profile upstream. The sewer main must be deep enough to allow for criteria relative to the laterals; 5 ft is usually the minimum depth.

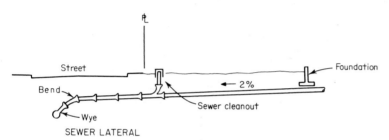

Fig. 7-5 Section showing lateral.

Where other criteria do not take precedence, the sewer should parallel the finished grade. Manholes should be shown at the locations required for the horizontal layout, at grade changes, and at 450-ft intervals—more frequently if required by the agency.

Keep in mind that a minimum velocity will be required to provide adequate scouring action. The minimum velocity will be based on criteria other than the pipe flowing at capacity. The size of the pipe and slope selected may provide sufficient velocity when flowing at capacity but not provide sufficient velocity during periods of average or less than average flow rates.

When designing sewer profiles be aware that when the slope changes, nonuniform flow may develop. Where the downstream slope is steeper, a drawdown curve may develop in the profile of the fluid surface. At the steeper slope the velocity will be greater, so the required area of cross section, that is, depth, will be less according to the continuity equations. A *draw-down curve* is the tapering of the longitudinal section. When the slope changes from a mild slope to a milder slope, the downstream section will be deeper and a *back-water curve* will develop. This, is a gradual increase in the longitudinal section. Ordinarily this nonuniform flow is not a problem.

However, if the design calls for a mild slope downstream of a steep slope, the shallow (supercritical) flow may become a deep (subcritical) flow and an hydraulic jump may develop. Sophisticated hydraulic calculations must be performed to understand the impact of the hydraulic jump. One solution to the problem is the installation of manholes to create a gradual change of slope. Manholes with outside drops (Fig. 7-11) can also be installed.

If vertical curves are allowed, use them in the profile where their use will avoid installation of one or more manholes. When they are to be used, they must be calculated as described in Chap. 6.

When a graphic representation of the profile is complete, the pipe sizes can be set. Many engineering firms now have programmed electronic calculators or computers that easily solve hydraulics problems using Manning's equation. But a circular slide rule designed to solve problems with Manning's equation is most commonly used.

Determining Pipe Sizes and Slopes

Before 1976, a circular slide rule designed specifically for making calculations using Manning's equation was available. The device was called a Feild's Hydraulics Calculator for Gravity Flow in Pipes. This calculator, or its successor, the Gravity Flow Hydraulics Calculator[5] (Fig. 7-6), is most often used in engineering offices for determining pipe sizes and slopes.

When one indicator on the calculator is lined up with the *n* value and another

---

[5]The Gravity Flow Hydraulics Calculator is available from the National Clay Pipe Institute (NCPI).

indicator is lined up with the flow rate, the following information for that value of n and that flow rate is displayed:

1. A range of pipe sizes and corresponding slopes available to accommodate the flow
2. The flow velocity for various pipe diameters
3. The flow rate, in millions of gallons per day, for various partial flows as indicated by liquid depth to pipe diameter ratios

By lining up an index opposite the velocity of flow in a full pipe, the velocity at various depths can be read. Most engineers find using the Feild's or NCPI calculators faster and easier than electronic calculators.

Example 7-3

Determine the size of pipe to use to transport 20 million gpd of sewage at a slope of 1 percent. Use 0.013 for Manning's n.

Fig. 7-6 Hydraulics calculator.

Solution

1. Align the flowrate, 20 million gpd (31 cfs), with the index for millions of gallons per day on the hydraulics calculator (Fig. 7-6).
2. Align the n value, 0.013, with the index for n on the calculator.
3. Find the value of 1 percent slope on the calculator. The calculator shows the slope as feet per 100 ft. Since this value is already a percentage, the percent slope is read directly. Opposite 1.0 on the slope scale is 27 in on the pipe diameter scale.

Calculating the Profile

Begin calculation of elevations, grades, and slopes at the outfall. The exact invert elevation should have been field-checked by a survey crew. Where the outfall is to be at an existing conduit rather than an existing manhole, the inverts at the manholes at either end of the existing conduit should be field-checked and an elevation for the proposed outfall calculated.

The connecting line must be equal or smaller in diameter. Whenever smaller pipes are connected, the overts (inside tops of pipes) are matched in elevation (Fig. 7-7).

Example 7-4

Determine the elevation of the invert for an 18-in conduit connecting to an existing 27-in conduit. The invert elevation of the 27-in sewer is 132.27.

Solution

1. Convert the pipe diameter to feet.

$$\frac{27 \text{ in}}{12 \text{ in/ft}} = 2.25 \text{ ft}$$

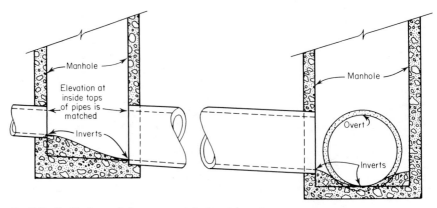

Fig. 7-7   Inside tops of pipes are matched, not inverts.

2. Determine the overt (inside top of pipe) elevation of the 27-in conduit.

$$132.27 \text{ ft} + 2.25 \text{ ft} = 134.52 \text{ ft}$$

The overts will be matched at elevation 134.52.

3. Convert 18 in to feet.

$$\frac{18 \text{ in}}{12 \text{ in/ft}} = 1.50 \text{ ft.}$$

4. The invert of the 18-in conduit will be 1.50 ft below the overt.

$$134.52 \text{ ft} - 1.50 \text{ ft} = 133.02 \text{ ft}$$

The elevation for the invert of the incoming 18-in line is 133.02.

This procedure is simplified by determining the difference in pipe diameters in feet and adding the differences to the invert of the larger pipe.

$$27 \text{ in} - 18 \text{ in} = 9 \text{ in} = 0.75 \text{ ft}$$
$$132.27 \text{ ft} + 0.75 \text{ ft} = 133.02 \text{ ft}$$

When calculating the slopes on conduits, care must be taken not to use the difference in stationing as the length of the conduit except where they are straight and parallel with the centerline. The length of the conduit must be measured or calculated from the plan view. If the sewer lines are straight where the centerline curves, the conduit will be shorter than the centerline. A conduit will also be shorter when it is concentric with and inside a centerline curve. It will be longer when it is concentric with and outside the centerline curve.

Example 7-5

Using Fig. 7-8, calculate the length of the sanitary sewer between centerline sta 5+00 and 8+92.70.

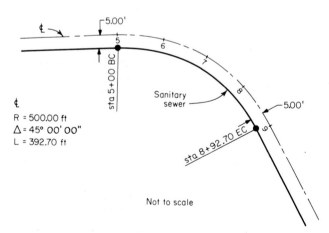

Fig. 7-8   Sewer length calculation for Example 7-5.

Solution

1. The determination of the length of the curve for the centerline and sewer is found with the same formula.

$$L_t = \frac{\Delta^\circ}{360^\circ}\pi 2R \qquad L_{ss} = \frac{\Delta^\circ}{360^\circ}\pi 2R_{ss}$$

$\dfrac{\Delta^\circ}{360^\circ}\pi 2$ is a constant in each curve with the same central angle (Δ°). Manipulating the equation algebraically gives

$$\frac{L}{R} = \frac{\Delta^\circ}{360^\circ}\pi 2 = K$$

$$\frac{L_{ss}}{R_{ss}} = \frac{\Delta^\circ}{360^\circ}\pi 2 = K$$

therefore

$$\frac{L}{R} = \frac{L_{ss}}{R_{ss}} = K \qquad\qquad (7\text{-}8)$$

$$\frac{L}{R} = \frac{392.70}{500} = 0.7854 = K$$

$$K = \frac{L_{ss}}{R_{ss}}$$

$$L_{ss} = K \times R_{ss} \qquad\qquad (7\text{-}9)$$
$$= 0.7854 \times 495.00 \text{ ft}$$
$$= 388.77 \text{ ft}$$

Once the constant for the value of the length divided by the radius for a particular central angle on the centerline curve is calculated, any other concentric curve with the same central angle (the storm sewer, the curbs, etc.) can be quickly calculated by multiplying the constant (K) by the radius of the sought after curve. The length of the sanitary sewer between sta 5+00 and 8+92.70 is 388.77 ft. The slope of the sewer between these stations is based on this distance. Label the actual lengths of the conduits on the profile.

To make an estimate of the slope on each section of conduit, scale the approximate elevations of the inverts at either end from the profile. Subtract the differences in elevations, and divide that difference by the length (Example 6-3). This yields the slope.

Determine the pipe sizes using the methods described earlier. Use the approximate slope just determined. The quantity (Q) to use for each section is the quantity at the outfall of each section of pipe. Each lateral connected to the main contributes to the quantity of sewage, but it is impractical to calculate and upgrade the main at each lateral. Therefore, a main of sufficient size to accommodate the flow from all the laterals between the two manholes is used.

Some jurisdictions require a drop between inverts where sewer mains connect. Determine if there is that requirement, and include the required drop wherever necessary.

Starting at the outfall invert, calculate the elevation at the upper end of the first section of pipe using the slope and length previously measured or calculated. The elevation of the invert at the lower end of the next upstream section is calculated as the invert elevation at the upper end of the first section plus the differences in pipe diameter or the drop requirement, whichever is larger. This process is continued upstream to the end.

Example 7-6

Determine invert elevations for the sewer pipes shown in Figure 7-9. A drop of 0.5 ft is required for connections at angles greater than 20°.

Solution

1. The invert elevation at the outfall, a 36-in conduit, is 261.04. The connecting pipe is 18 in.

$$36 \text{ in} - 18 \text{ in} = 18 \text{ in} = 1.5 \text{ ft}$$
$$261.04 \text{ ft} + 1.50 \text{ ft} = 262.54 \text{ ft}$$

2. Multiply the length of the next section of pipe times the slope.

$$203 \text{ ft} \times 0.004 = 0.81 \text{ ft}$$

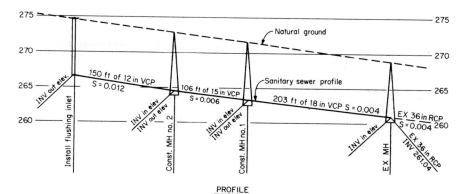

Fig. 7-9 Plan and profile for Example 7-6.

Add 0.81 to the downstream invert.

$$262.54 \text{ ft} + 0.81 \text{ ft} = 263.35 \text{ ft}$$

Thus 263.35 is the invert of the upstream end of the 18-in pipe.

3. The next upstream section of pipe enters manhole no. 1 at an angle of 22°. A 0.50-ft drop is required. The incoming pipe at manhole no. 1 has a 15-in diameter.

$$18 \text{ in} - 15 \text{ in} = 3 \text{ in} = 0.25 \text{ ft}$$
$$0.50 \text{ ft} > 0.25 \text{ ft}$$

The drop requirement exceeds the size difference. Add 0.50 ft to the downstream invert.

$$263.35 \text{ ft} + 0.50 \text{ ft} = 263.85 \text{ ft}$$

4. Multiply the length of the next upstream section of pipe times the slope, and add the product to the downstream invert.

$$106.00 \text{ ft} \times 0.006 = 0.64 \text{ ft}$$
$$263.85 \text{ ft} + 0.64 \text{ ft} = 264.49 \text{ ft}$$

The upstream invert elevation of the 15-in line is 264.49.

5. The next upstream section of pipe is 12 in.

$$15 \text{ in} - 12 \text{ in} = 3 \text{ in} = 0.25 \text{ ft.}$$

There is no drop requirement. Add 0.25 ft to the invert of the 15-in pipe at manhole no. 2 for the invert of the 12-in pipe.

$$264.49 \text{ ft} + 0.25 \text{ ft} = 264.74 \text{ ft}$$

6. Multiply the length of the next section by the slope, and add the product to the invert.

$$150.00 \text{ ft} \times 0.012 = 1.80 \text{ ft}$$
$$264.74 \text{ ft} + 1.80 \text{ ft} = 266.54 \text{ ft}$$

The invert elevation at the flushing inlet is 266.54.

Example 7-7

Using a Feild's or NCPI calculator, determine the pipe size and slope to use for a flow rate of 12 cfs. The upstream conduit will be 12 in. The downstream conduit, which is the outfall, is 18 in. The requirements of the sanitation district are:

Minimum slope, 0.004
Minimum pipe size, 8 in
Velocity 2 fps min., 10 fps max.
Manning's $n = 0.013$

Solution

1. Align the flow rate, 12 cfs, with the index for cfs on the hydraulics calculator.
2. Align the n value, 0.013, with the index for n on the calculator.
3. Determine the range of sizes of pipe that can be used.
   a. The mark for the minimum slope allowed (0.004) is between 21 and 24 on the

scale for pipe diameters (Fig. 7-10a). Notice that the slope on the calculator is shown as feet per 100 ft, not feet per foot. If the minimum slope is selected, a 24-in pipe is required.

b. The mark for the minimum velocity, 2 fps, is opposite 33 on the pipe diameter scale (Fig. 7-10b). The required slope when using a 33-in pipe is 0.0005 (Fig. 7-10c). Pipes with smaller diameters placed on a steeper slope will provide greater velocities. The maximum velocity, 10 fps, occurs in a 15-in-diameter pipe (Fig. 7-10d). To satisfy velocity requirements, a pipe with a diameter between 15 and 33 in must be used.

c. The next downstream conduit is 18 in. Regardless of hydraulic requirements, each successive downstream conduit in a piping network must be larger than the last to prevent clogging of the lines. The conduit must not be larger than the outfall. To satisfy maintenance requirements, an 18-in-diameter pipe or smaller must be used.

   The velocity requirement limits the pipe diameter to between 15 and 33 in. The minimum slope required a 24-in or larger pipe. These two requirements narrow the range of pipe sizes to between 15 and 24 in. The maintenance

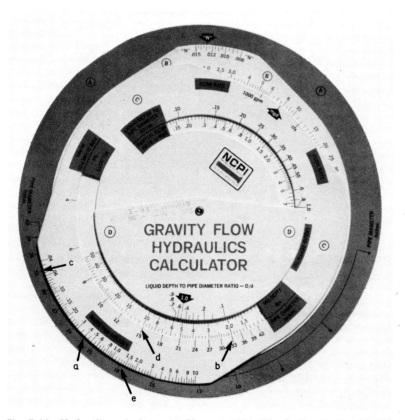

Fig. 7-10 Hydraulics calculator. (a) Slope at 0.004; (b) velocity of 2 fps; (c) 33-in pipe; (d) 10 fps; (e) 18-in pipe.

requirement limits the pipe to 18 in or smaller. The acceptable range of sizes is now narrowed to two—15 or 18 in. The upstream pipe is 12 in, so either a 15- or 18-in-diameter pipe will be acceptable from the maintenance standpoint.
4. Opposite the 15-in-diameter pipe index on the hydraulics calculator is a slope of 0.034; opposite the 18-in pipe is a slope of 0.0125 (Fig. 7-10e).
5. The requirements of the profile may prescribe which pipe to use. If not, use the smaller conduit as it will be cheaper.

Manholes and Flushing Inlets

Maintenance of the sewer network is necessary, so manholes are installed at regular intervals and at potential trouble spots—where the direction of flow changes either horizontally or vertically and where connections are made. A manhole or flushing inlet should also be installed at the end of the line. The jurisdiction should have standard plans and specifications for manholes and flushing inlets.

Manholes are typically 4 or 5 ft in diameter and are topped by a cone (Fig. 7-11). Grading rings may be placed on top of the cone then the frame and cover.[6] To protect the health and safety of maintenance personnel, conduits should connect no higher than 2.5 ft above the bottom of the manhole. If this is impractical, an outside drop should be constructed (Fig. 7-11).

[6]Manhole covers are round so that they cannot be dropped into the manhole and so that there is less likelihood of their rattling when driven over.

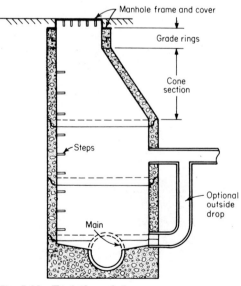

Fig. 7-11   Typical manhole.

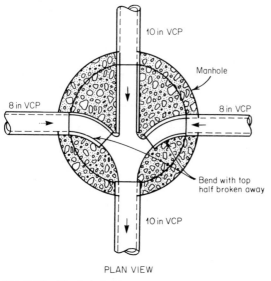

10 in VCP

Manhole

8 in VCP

8 in VCP

Bend with top
half broken away

10 in VCP

PLAN VIEW

Fig. 7-12 Manhole bottom.

The inside bottom of sanitary manholes should be shaped to ensure smooth flow of the sewage. One way to accomplish this is by setting bends of sewer conduits in the concrete (Fig. 7-12). When the concrete has hardened, the top half of the pipe is broken out and connections are made smooth with cement.

When several conduits are to enter one manhole, draw a plan view and a cross-sectional view at a large scale, such as 1 in = 2 ft, to check that there is sufficient surface to accommodate the conduits.

The end of sanitary sewer lines should be equipped with a manhole or flushing inlet (Fig. 7-3) to allow maintenance crews to check for breaks and to flush out the lines.

PRESSURE SYSTEMS

When existing sanitary sewer outfalls are too high for the design of a gravity-flow system, a pumped system must be used. First a gravity-flow system is designed to accommodate the flow while keeping the pipes as shallow as possible. At the lower end of the system, a manhole or wet well is installed. A force main (pressure system) is then designed to carry the sewage from the manhole at the low end of the system to an available outfall. The force mains (FM) may parallel the gravity system or may be located elsewhere. A pumping station is located at either the upper or lower end of the force main.

SEPTIC TANKS

In areas where a sanitary sewer system is not available, septic tanks may be allowed for individual residences or for buildings with small amounts of sewage. The soil must be tested to determine if the percolation rate can provide adequate dissipation of liquids. The minimum size of tank and leach field will be dictated by local health departments.

REFERENCES

American Society of Civil Engineers and the Water Pollution Control Federation: *Design and Construction of Sanitary and Storm Sewers,* American Society of Civil Engineers, New York, 1968.

Brater, E. F., and King, Horace: *Handbook of Hydraulics,* McGraw-Hill Book Co., New York, 1976.

Metcalf & Eddy, Inc.: *Wastewater Engineering,* McGraw-Hill Book Co., New York, 1972.

National Clay Pipe Institute: *Clay Pipe Engineering Manual,* National Clay Pipe Institute, Washington, DC, 1982.

Chapter Eight

Storm Drainage

On every site attention must be given to the storm water impacts. Precipitation falls on the site in the form of rain, hail, or snow, and runoff flows through the site. Storm drainage facilities must be designed to protect people and property from storm water inundation. Designing the storm drainage system requires an understanding of *hydrology* (the science of the natural occurrence, distribution, and circulation of the water on the earth and in the atmosphere), *hydraulics* (the science of the mechanics of fluids at rest and in motion), and drainage law. Understanding the elements of the design of storm facilities and their coordination with surface improvements and underground utilities is essential. Drainage law varies from location to location, so local drainage laws must be investigated and applied.

HYDROLOGY

A formal study of hydrology includes complicated concepts of weather forecasting, storm water runoff, and steam flow routing, as well as the determination of groundwater characteristics. Fortunately, however, for the small areas ordinarily encountered in private land development, the rational formula provides a conservative flow rate that can be used for designing storm water facilities. The rational formula is shown in Eq. 8-1.

$$Q = CIA \qquad (8\text{-}1)$$

where Q = flow rate, cfs
C = runoff coefficient
I = rainfall intensity, in/h
A = area, acres

NOTE: Inches per hour times acres does not yield cubic feet per second. However, the conversion factor gives a constant of 1.008 which most engineers ignore.

$$C \times I \frac{in}{h} \times \frac{h}{3600 \ sec} \times \frac{ft}{12 \ in} \times A \ acre \times \frac{43560 \ ft^2}{acre} = 1.008 \ cfs$$

Rainfall Intensity

The intensity factor (I) of the rational formula is the rate of rainfall over the area in inches per hour. This factor can be taken from an Intensity-Duration-Frequency (IDF) chart supplied by the responsible agency (Fig. 8-1).

To find the intensity from the chart, you must know the return period. If the return period is 100 years, the rate of rainfall given is of the most intense storm during a 100-year period. This is called a "100-year storm." If the return period is 10 years, the rate of rainfall is of the most intense storm during a 10-year period and is called a "10-year storm." The greater the interval, the greater the intensity. The jurisdiction responsible for flood control will dictate what return period to use to determine the intensity. This will be exemplified later in this chapter.

The duration is the amount of time it takes for a drop of rain to travel from

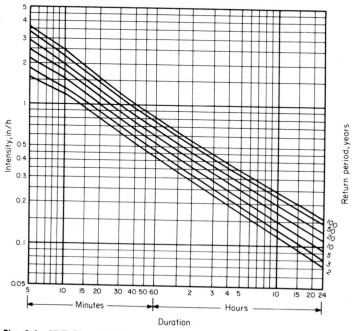

Fig. 8-1 IDF Chart for San Jose, CA.

the most distant point in the drainage basin (described below) to the drainage structure. This is called the *time of concentration* (t_c). There are complicated formulas[1] to determine the time of concentration, but for the small-scale hydrologic problems involved in ordinary subdivision and site development work, an estimate of the duration is adequate. If the distance is from the rooftop to the curb and gutter, 10 to 15 min can be used. Here the most distant point in the drainage basin is judged to be the rooftop. The gutter is the drainage structure. The time of concentration increases as the drop of rain continues downstream.

If you have the return period, say 5 years, and duration, say 15 min, the intensity can be read from an IDF chart. To determine the intensity from Fig. 8-1, first find the return period of 5 years on the right-hand side of the chart. The 5 is at the end of a diagonal line. Now, find the duration of 15 min at the bottom of the chart. Follow the vertical line representing 15 min until it intersects the diagonal line for the 5-year return period. The intersection falls about halfway between the horizontal line for 1 and 1.5 in/h. The resulting intensity is 1.25 in/h. Notice that as the duration gets longer, the intensity diminishes. The reason for the decrease in intensity is that peak intensity is seldom sustained for long. The average intensity is less for longer periods of time.

Storm Water Runoff

The runoff coefficient (C) of the formula represents the amount of water running off as a proportion of the total amount of precipitation falling on the area. Of the precipitation reaching the ground, some will percolate into the soil, some will be taken up by the vegetative cover, some will evaporate, and the remaining will run off. For streets, the coefficients range from 0.70 to 0.95. That is, 70 to 95 percent of the precipitation falling on the area will run off. The responsible agency may have a table of coefficients to use. Table 8-1 can be used when the design frequency is 5 to 10 years. The coefficient reflects the type of soil, type of ground cover, and the evenness and degree of slope. Typically, the area will consist of more than one type of cover, and a weighted average should be used.

Example 8-1

Determine the runoff coefficient for an area that is 65 percent paving and buildings and 35 percent landscaping.

Solution

1. Obtain the runoff coefficients from Table 8-1 for paving (streets), $C = 0.95$, and landscaping (lawns), $C = 0.22$.

---

[1]An example can be found in Linsley, Ray K., and Franzini, Joseph B.: *Water Resources Engineering*, 2d ed., McGraw-Hill Book Co., New York, 1972, pp. 58–59.

2. Calculate a weighted average.

C		Portion of Area		
0.95	$\times$	0.65	$=$	0.62
0.22	$\times$	0.35	$=$	$+0.08$
			$C =$	0.70

TABLE 8-1 Typical *C* Values for 5- to 10-Year Frequency Design*

Description of Area	Runoff Coefficients
Business	
Downtown areas	0.70–0.95
Neighborhood areas	0.50–0.70
Residential	
Single-family areas	0.30–0.50
Multiunits, detached	0.40–0.60
Multiunits, attached	0.60–0.75
Residential (suburban)	0.25–0.40
Apartment dwelling areas	0.50–0.70
Industrial	
Light areas	0.50–0.80
Heavy areas	0.60–0.90
Parks, cemeteries	0.10–0.25
Playgrounds	0.20–0.35
Railroad yard areas	0.20–0.40
Unimproved areas	0.10–0.30
Streets	
Asphaltic	0.70–0.95
Concrete	0.80–0.95
Brick	0.70–0.85
Drives and walks	0.75–0.85
Roofs	0.75–0.85
Lawns, sandy soil	
Flat, 2%	0.05–0.10
Average, 2 to 7%	0.10–0.15
Steep, 7%	0.15–0.20
Lawns, heavy soil	
Flat, 2%	0.13–0.17
Average, 2 to 7%	0.18–0.22
Steep, 7%	0.25–0.35

*Taken from Viessman, Jr., Warren, Harhaugh, Terrence E., and Knapp, John W.: *Introduction to Hydrology,* Intext Educational Publishers, New York, p. 306, 1972.

Note that in Table 8-1 improved areas yield more runoff—i.e., have higher values of *C*—than unimproved areas. Because of this, developing an area with buildings and streets increases the runoff. Consequently, storm systems that have previously been adequate, may become overloaded as the land is developed.

When downstream drainage facilities are inadequate, retention ponds can be used to mitigate the problem. *Retention ponds* are small-scale flood control reservoirs. The purpose of these ponds is to catch and detain storm runoff. Ordinarily, the pond is designed so that the amount of runoff that the downstream drainage facilities can accommodate is released, while the excess runoff is held back and released at a controlled rate. The calculation of the capacity necessary for a retention pond should be done by a hydrologist and is beyond the scope of this book.

Determination of the Area

The area (A) of the rational formula is the area of the drainage basin. A *drainage basin* is that area of land from which drainage contributes to a particular waterway. When the waterway referred to is a river, the area is called a *river basin*. A river basin is made up of small, tributary drainage basins.

Several drainage basins are illustrated in Fig. 8-2. Ridges W, X, Y, and Z and swales A, B, and C are shown. Drainage basin A is bounded by ridges W, X, and Y and contributes storm water to swale A. Drainage basin B is bounded by ridges Y and Z; water falling there contributes to swale B. To determine the amount of runoff reaching the point of concentration at A, delineate the drainage basin contributing to that point in the swale (waterway). Water flowing overland follows the steepest route. The flow line of the steepest route will always be perpendicular to the contours. To delineate the drainage basin contributing to a particular point, trace the flow line, from point A, up the contours at right angles (Fig. 8-2).

Drainage basins in a developed area are shown in Fig. 8-3. One drainage area is bounded on the north by the crown on "A" Street, on the south by the lot

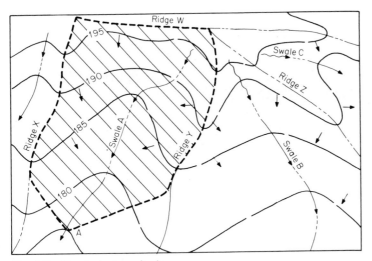

Fig. 8-2 Simple drainage basins.

line between lots 2 through 5 and 8 through 11, and east and west by ridges through lots 1 and 6. This drainage area is collected at catch basin A. Catch basin B collects water from the area bounded by the ridges described above through lots 1 to 11 and by the crowns on First Street, Second Street, and "B" Street.

The first step in a drainage system design is developing the site grading plan (Chap. 5). The on-site surface drainage basins are created by runoff that is directed to ditches and storm water inlets.

Six of the lots shown in Fig. 8-3 will interface with existing drainage basins along the northerly tract boundary. In this case, the lots will be graded so that the north half of each drains north and the south half drains to "A" Street. First and Second Streets slope south. Two of the drainage basins established when the lots are constructed this way are delineated in Fig. 8-3. The storm water falling on the basins will be collected in the ditch along the northerly tract boundary and picked up by field inlets (FI) no. 1 and no. 2. The ditch here must be designed to accommodate the off-site drainage basins to the north as well.

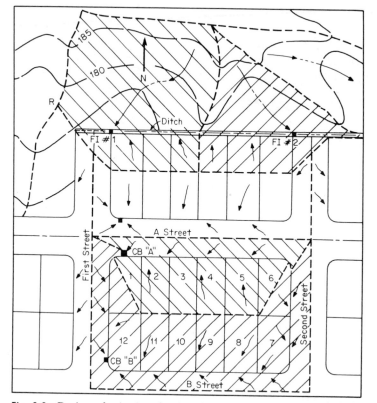

Fig. 8-3   Drainage basins in a developed area.

Notice that the runoff flows perpendicular to the contour lines, as is shown by the flow lines. At the northwest corner of the tract, the basin is limited by the point the water flows from. Water falling south of point R flows south and will not reach the site. Therefore, the limit of the basin is as shown. When the boundaries of the drainage basins are defined, their areas can be calculated. If the drainage basin is irregular, use a planimeter as described in Chap. 5. Convert the area to acres before putting it into the rational formula. When the quantity of runoff (Q) is established, the size and type of drainage facilities can be designed.

Small Individual Sites

Individual sites are graded to drain storm water overland to the street whenever possible. When this cannot be done, the parking lots and landscaped areas are graded to create drainage basins. At low points, the water is collected in storm water inlets. The inlets are then connected to a piping network. If the lot is small, some agencies will allow a 3-in pipe or a set of 3-in pipes to be connected to the inlet and routed through the curb into the gutter, rather than into a piping system. Of course, there must be enough fall to provide sufficient slope and the basin must be small enough for a 3-in pipe or pipes to have sufficient capacity.

Dry wells can be used to drain small basins or localized ponding where connection to an underground system is impractical. A *dry well* is a hole filled with gravel or other permeable rock. The runoff can be stored beneath the surface in the interstices of the gravel while it percolates into the ground. If it is in a landscaped area, the rock may be left exposed or may be overlaid with lawn. If it is in a paved area, a storm water inlet will be installed at the low point and openings will be made to allow drainage from the inlet to the rock. If the groundwater table is high because of a layer of impermeable soil, the well must be deep enough to reach below the impermeable layer.

SURFACE IMPROVEMENTS AND STRUCTURES

Surface improvements for controlling storm water are grading, ditches, and storm water inlets. The method of designing grading to provide drainage is described in Chaps. 5 and 6.

Ditches

When runoff from an unimproved area reaches the site as overland flow, it must be intercepted and collected. This can be accomplished with ditches. As with sewers, the amount of runoff determines the design of the ditch.

When the drainage basins are very small (less than 0.25 acres), a simple note

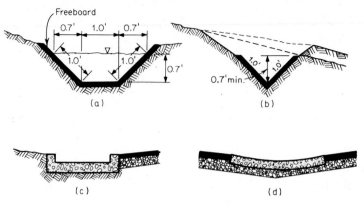

Fig. 8-4 Types of ditches. (*a*) Trapezoidal; (*b*) "V" ditch; (*c*) flat-bottomed ditch; (*d*) curved ditch.

"grade to drain," at the flow line of the ditch on the plan may be sufficient for construction. Unlined ditches can be used when their slopes are greater than 0.02. In time, an unlined ditch will become irregular and not flow if the slope is less than 0.02. If conditions require a shallow slope, use a concrete-lined ditch with a minimum slope of 0.003.

The allowable steepness for an earthen ditch is dependent upon the erodibility of the soil and the velocity of the flowrate. Where erosion will be a problem, the ditch can be lined with any one of a number of materials. Asphalt, concrete, Gunite, and cobblestones are a few. Economics and velocities will indicate which one is best.

The cross section of the ditch is designed to fit the circumstances and accommodate the flow (Fig. 8-4). A "V" ditch is most economical. If the ditch is located where people are likely to step into it, a shallow, flat bottomed, or curved ditch is better. If the ditch is to carry a large Q, a trapezoidal ditch is more efficient.

To determine the required cross-sectional area of the ditch, use the equation

$$A_R = \frac{Q}{V} \tag{8-2}$$

where A_R = cross-sectional area required, ft^2
Q = quantity, cfs
V = velocity, fps

Q is determined by Eq. 8-1. Velocity is determined with Manning's equation:

$$V = \frac{1.486}{n} R_H^{2/3} S^{1/2} \tag{8-3}$$

where n = the coefficient of friction

R_H = hydraulic radius, $\dfrac{\text{area}}{\text{wetted perimeter}}$, $\dfrac{a}{p}$

S = slope, feet per foot

The responsible jurisdiction may have a table of values of n, a surface rough-ness factor, for different surfaces. Otherwise, use Table 8-2. The hydraulic radius is the cross-sectional area of the ditch divided by the wetted perimeter. The *wetted perimeter* is the length of the surface on the cross section that will be wet when the ditch is at design capacity (Example 8-2). The slope is that of the ditch profile.

To design the ditch profile, draw a groundline profile at the centerline or edges of the ditch. Draw a line roughly parallel with and below the lowest ground line profile (Fig. 8-5). The ditch profile must be below the ground at least as far as the ditch is deep. That is, if the ditch is 1 ft deep, the flow line profile must be at least 1 ft below the natural ground at the edge. Otherwise, the ditch will come out of the ground. Make no more breaks in the profile than are necessary to accommodate the changes in the groundline profile. If the cross slope is steep or erratic, it may be necessary to draw cross sections at critical points to verify that cut slopes will daylight within the property or within a reasonable distance. When the ditch profile is drawn, calculate the slope as described in Chap. 6.

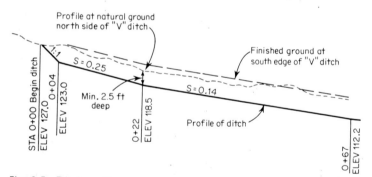

Fig. 8-5 Ditch profile.

Example 8-2

Calculate the hydraulic radius R_H for Fig. 8-4a.

Solution

1. Add the lengths of the surfaces on the cross section that will be wet when flowing at design capacity.

$$p = 1 \text{ ft} + 1 \text{ ft} + 1 \text{ ft} = 3 \text{ ft}$$

TABLE 8-2 Values of *n* to Be Used with Manning's Equation*

Surface	Best	Good	Fair	Bad
Uncoated cast-iron pipe	0.012	0.013	0.014	0.015
Coated cast-iron pipe	0.011	0.012†	0.013†	
Commercial wrought-iron pipe, black	0.012	0.013	0.014	0.015
Commercial wrought-iron pipe, galvanized	0.013	0.014	0.015	0.017
Polyvinyl chloride (PVC) pipe	0.009	0.010	0.011	
Smooth brass and glass pipe	0.009	0.010	0.011	0.013
Smooth lockbar and welded "OD" pipe	0.010	0.011†	0.013†	
Riveted and spiral steel pipe	0.013	0.015†	0.017†	
Vitrified sewer pipe	$\begin{Bmatrix} 0.010 \\ 0.011 \end{Bmatrix}$	0.013†	0.015	0.017
Common clay drainage tile	0.011	0.012†	0.014†	0.017
Glazed brickwork	0.011	0.012	0.013†	0.015
Brick in cement mortar; brick sewers	0.012	0.013	0.015†	0.017
Canals and ditches				
Earth, straight and uniform	0.017	0.020	0.0225†	0.025
Rock cuts, smooth and uniform	0.025	0.030	0.033†	0.035
Rock cuts, jagged and irregular	0.035	0.040	0.045	
Winding sluggish canals	0.0225	0.025†	0.0275	0.030
Dredged earth channels	0.025	0.0275	0.030	0.033
Canals with rough stony beds, weeds on earth banks	0.025	0.030	0.035†	0.040
Earth bottom, rubber sides	0.028	0.030†	0.033†	0.035
Natural stream channels				
1. Clean, straight bank, full stage no rifts or deep pools	0.025	0.0275	0.030	0.033
2. Same as 1, but some weeds and stones	0.030	0.033	0.035	0.040
3. Winding, some pools and shoals, clean	0.033	0.035	0.040	0.045
4. Same as 3, lower stages, more ineffective slopes and sections	0.040	0.045	0.050	0.055
Neat cement surfaces	0.010	0.011	0.012	0.013
Cement mortar surfaces	0.011	0.012	0.013†	0.015
Concrete pipe	0.012	0.013	0.015†	0.016
Wood stave pipe	0.010	0.011	0.012	0.013
Plank flumes				
Planed	0.010	0.012†	0.013	0.014
Unplaned	0.011	0.013†	0.014	0.015
With battens	0.012	0.015†	0.016	
Concrete-lined channels	0.012	0.014†	0.016†	0.018
Cement-rubble surface	0.017	0.020	0.025	0.030
Dry-rubble surface	0.025	0.030	0.033	0.035
Dressed-ashlar surface	0.013	0.014	0.015	0.017
Semicircular metal flumes, smooth	0.011	0.012	0.013	0.015
Semicircular metal flumes, corrugated	0.0225	0.025	0.0275	0.030
5. Same as 3, some weeds and stones	0.035	0.040	0.045	0.050
6. Same as 4, stony sections	0.045	0.050	0.055	0.060
7. Sluggish river reaches, rather weedy or with very deep pools	0.050	0.060	0.070	0.080
8. Very weedy reaches	0.075	0.100	0.125	0.150

*Adapted from Brater and King, pp. 7–22.
†Values commonly used in designing.

2. Calculate the cross-sectional area of the ditch when it is flowing at design capacity.

$$a = \frac{b_1 + b_2}{2} h$$
$$= \frac{(0.7 + 1.0 + 0.7) + 1}{2} \times 0.7 \text{ ft}$$
$$= 1.19 \text{ ft}^2$$

3. Calculate R_H

$$R_H = \frac{a}{p} = \frac{1.19}{3} = 0.40$$

If the slopes exceed 0.01, the design of the ditch may be shown entirely on the cross section by showing a minimum depth below existing ground for the flow line of the ditch, as shown in Fig. 8-4b. The grading contractor can then cut the ditch without the need of survey stakes for vertical control. If the design requires more exact vertical control, flow line or ditch centerline elevations can be shown on the grading plan or the plan view of the construction plans at grade breaks. This way ditch profiles do not have to be drawn on the finished plans.

When a slope has been selected, use it in Manning's equation (Eq. 8-3) to calculate V. Now, divide V into Q_R (Eq. 8-2) to get the cross-sectional area required. Compare the area required with the area the ditch section provides. If the cross-sectional area of the ditch is larger, the design will work; if not, try using a larger cross section and/or steeper slope. Then go through the procedure again using the new R_H and/or S (Fig. 8-6). If the ditch is long and/or lined and the section is much larger than necessary, it is advisable to make the cross section smaller, thus cheaper. Here again, if the design of the cross section is changed, a new a and a new p must be determined and R_H recalculated.

Storm Water Inlets

At the low point in the ditch, the water is collected and routed underground. To accomplish this, a storm water inlet is used (Fig. 8-7). If the inlet is going

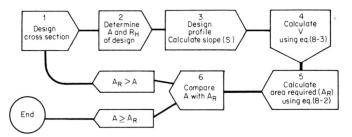

Fig. 8-6 Flow chart for ditch design.

to be on public property, the approving public agency should have standard plans showing what to use. On private property, choose an inlet from a catalog of locally available, prefabricated products whenever possible. By identifying the inlet as "'Christy' inlet no. 241 or equivalent," the contractor will be given some flexibility. If the size and shape of the ditch will not accommodate the inlet chosen, show a transition to a cross section that fits the inlet.

In situations where there are very large flows to be collected, verify that the inlet opening has sufficient capacity. The agency or inlet manufacturer should have specifications of the inlet capacity. If the information is not available, calculate capacity. There is a description of how to accomplish this in Linsley and Franzini, pp. 511–517.

Verify that there is enough space in the walls of the inlet to accommodate the pipes entering and/or leaving. Where the pipe enters on the skew, make a large scale (1 in = 2 ft) sketch of the plan view (Fig. 8-8). If two pipes enter the same side of an inlet, a cross-sectional sketch may be helpful.

Manholes

A cross section of a typical manhole is shown in Fig. 7-11. Note the cone on top. It serves to reduce the opening diameter so a 2-ft-diameter manhole cover can

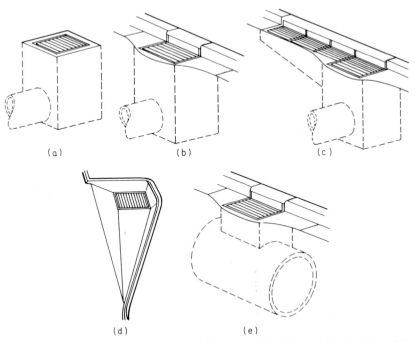

Fig. 8-7 Types of storm water inlets. (*a*) Flat grate inlet; (*b*) catch basin; (*c*) catch basin with gallery; (*d*) offset inlet; (*e*) catch basin over large storm main.

be used over a 4- to 5-ft-diameter manhole. An eccentric cone can be useful in cases where the manhole is located directly under some obstacle on the surface, such as on the curb and gutter. The cone can be rotated away from the obstacle. The tops of pipes on incoming lines must be below the cone. If the line is unusually shallow and this is not possible, a custom manhole must be designed. When an incoming line enters with the invert more than 2.5 ft above the bottom of the manhole, an outside drop (Fig. 7-11) should be used.

Some manholes will have several lines entering. Verify that there is sufficient space in the walls of the manhole for pipes to enter without intersecting other pipes by making a 1 in = 2 ft scale plan view drawing and a cross section. A very complicated manhole may require a plan of the interior surface of the manhole; it should be cut vertically and laid out with each connection drawn on. The invert elevations are critical in these cases. If there is not enough space, the manhole must be relocated or a manhole added.

THE SEWER NETWORK

Complicated criteria are applied to the design of the piping system: agency requirements, physical laws of hydraulics, coordination with new and existing facilities, construction technology, and cost considerations.

The agency may dictate criteria such as horizontal locations, depth, velocity of flow and/or minimum slopes, minimum pipe sizes, types, and classes. The agency should have a master storm drainage plan of all the storm runoff

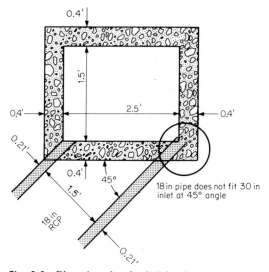

Fig. 8-8 Plan view sketch of 18-in pipe entering storm water inlet. Check for fit.

requirements in the area and may dictate pipes large enough to accommodate future growth. Usually construction specifications and standard plans of facilities are dictated. The agency may set a criterion as to how much runoff can be carried in the streets. The criterion is usually expressed as the distance that the runoff may flow in the gutters before it must be picked up.

Locating Inlets

Catch basins will be located at the low points in streets, at the low points of intersections, usually at one end of curb returns, and at intervals to satisfy the other criteria stated above. If the criterion is a specified width of gutter flow, treat the gutter the same as a ditch. The available gutter width determines a modified "V" ditch. The dimensions and cross-sectional area are known from the required street section. The longitudinal slope is the street's slope.

Some agencies allow the use of valley gutters (Fig. 8-9). The valley gutter transfers the gutter flow from one side of a secondary street to the other, thereby eliminating the need of at least one catch basin and some sewer lines. When a valley gutter is used, set the elevations at the points marked on Fig. 8-9 to ensure that there will be no ponding.

When the allowable overland flow reaches the limiting criterion, the runoff must be picked up. Ordinarily, pickup will be made with a catch basin. All the locations of catch basins must be determined before the sewer network can be laid out.

Coordinating Facilities

When the grading plan has been designed and ditches and catch basins have been located, the underground network of storm sewers can be laid out. The storm lines must be coordinated with the sanitary system as well as with the grading. Because of this, a project master plan including all three, the grading

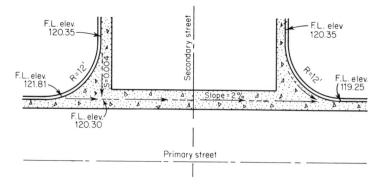

Fig. 8-9 Plan view of concrete valley gutter.

plan, the sanitary sewers, and the storm sewers, is needed. Other facilities, new or existing, that will require accommodation should also be shown. This master plan should be drawn at a scale that can include the entire project. Usually, a copy of the tentative map or preliminary grading plan makes a good base map.

To design the system, all available outfalls must be identified. An *outfall* is the place where the sewer discharges. It may be a river, channel, stream, lake, or, most commonly, a sewer main. To be available, the outfall must have unused capacity and an invert elevation low enough to accommodate the new system. Write the invert elevations on the master plan to use later to coordinate crossings. The capacity required will be based on the runoff from all the drainage basins contributing to it.

When laying out and coordinating the sewer systems, keep in mind what will be most economical and most expedient. Plot the locations and elevations of all the storm and sanitary outfalls that are available. When more than one outfall is used, the total length and required diameter of resulting mains will be less. Plotting all the outfalls shows what flexibility there is.

Decide whether the storm or the sanitary sewer system has more critical restraints. If the fall across the site is 1 percent (1 ft per 100 ft) or greater and the inverts of both storm and sanitary outfalls are greater than 6 ft deep, it may not be clear which sewer is more critical. In this case, the sanitary system should be laid out first.

Some agencies dictate the horizontal locations of storm and sanitary lines, e.g., "storm mains must be installed five feet north or east of the centerline of the street." If the horizontal location of the sewer main is not specified, consider what will be most economical. If there are more sanitary laterals on one side of the street than on the other, place the sanitary main on that side of the street. This way, more of the laterals will be shorter from the property line to the main, and there will be fewer sanitary laterals crossing the storm main.

Consider locations that minimize crossings. In Fig. 8-10*a*, the sanitary mains are located on the north and east sides of the streets and the storm mains are located on the south and west sides. Here, there is a crossing point in the southeast quadrant. In this example, if the storm main is placed south and east and

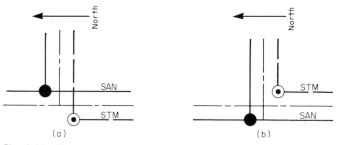

Fig. 8-10 Horizontal layout of sewers.

the sanitary main is placed north and west, that crossing can be eliminated (Fig. 8-10b). Not only is that one less crossing clearance to calculate, but, more importantly, there is one less potential trouble spot if there is a design or construction discrepancy.

When laying out the storm main on the plan view, curves are sometimes allowed. The allowable degree of deflection or radius of curvature is specified by the pipe manufacturer. Some agencies do not allow curved mains; others do under specific circumstances such as where a manhole is provided at the BC and/or EC. When curves are to be used, exact locations of the BC and EC as well as curve data must be calculated before the design is complete.

Designing the Storm Sewer Profile

When the horizontal location is complete, design of the profile can begin. The actual design will be done on a profile worksheet. The profile should show all existing factors: the underground electrical and telephone lines and all crossings. Often there is more than one conduit for each utility. At crossings, both the top and bottom of conduits should be shown. In streets that have been used for many years, the utilities may form a vertical curtain along the street. It is important that a thorough search be made to show all underground utilities or other obstacles to the main and its appurtenances. Show critical points, such as utility crossings, and design the profile to clear them.

Always begin from the outfall and project the profile upstream. Use inverts that are sufficiently above the sanitary lines to allow the top of the sanitary lateral to clear the bottom of the storm main. Some agencies require a minimum amount of clearance. The inverts of the mains must be deep enough so that the top of the storm water laterals are below the street subgrade at the back of the curb or edge of the pavement (Fig. 8-11). This serves two purposes; by putting the pipes below the roadwork, they are protected from being ripped out by construction equipment, and the subgrade distributes the traffic loads, protecting the pipes from being crushed. The class of pipe to use should be selected from the manufacturer's specifications to withstand expected traffic loads. A concrete cap can be poured over pipes where additional protection is needed for shallow pipes or where pipe crossings have little clearance (Fig. 8-12). Cast-iron pipe can be used in extreme cases.

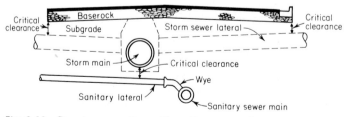

Fig. 8-11 Street cross section with sanitary sewer deeper.

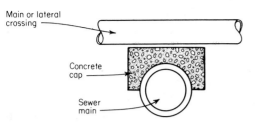

Fig. 8-12   Concrete cap.

If the sanitary main is shallow or the storm line is larger than 30 in, it may be necessary to design the storm line profile below the sanitary line (Fig. 8-13). Here, storm laterals must clear the sanitary main. If manholes are required at the storm lateral connections, the storm laterals can then go over the sanitary main and clearance should not be a problem.

On commercial and industrial sites, as well as on some residential sites, there will be storm water inlets on the lots. In this case, the mains must be deep enough so that the tops of the laterals at the storm water inlet have enough cover. If the end of the lateral is in a paved area, the top of the lateral should be below the subgrade. If the lateral is in a landscaped area, it should be at least a foot deep so that gardening equipment will not damage it.

When the profile changes horizontal or vertical direction and when the pipe size changes, a manhole is usually required. A manhole is also required at intervals of 500 ft or less to facilitate maintenance. Where downstream slopes are steeper, a smaller diameter line can accommodate the same flow. Regardless of the hydraulic requirements, however, the pipe size should always be the same or smaller than the next downstream section to prevent clogging of the line.

The agency will dictate vertical criteria. For example, "The top of pipe must be two feet below the top of curb," or "The hydraulic grade line must be a minimum of six inches below the top of curb for the 100 year storm." Identify critical points on the profile, such as crossings and changes of slope in the street profile. Keep in mind the criteria stated earlier about laterals. Where no other

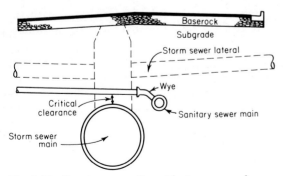

Fig. 8-13   Street cross section with storm sewer deeper.

factors govern, keep the pipe as shallow as possible in order to keep down the cost of trenching and depths of manholes. However, where connecting to deep manholes, the invert should be no higher than 2.5 ft above the bottom of the manhole to avoid the cost of an outside drop.

Ordinarily, the agency will dictate the range of acceptable flow velocities. The velocities determine minimum and maximum slopes. If the agency has not dictated velocities, use a minimum of 2 fps and a maximum of 10 fps. In a 12-in-diameter concrete pipe, a slope of 0.003 yields 2 fps; a slope of 0.064 yields 10 fps.

Determining Pipe Sizes

Calculation of the size of pipe required to accommodate a single drainage basin is simple. All that is needed is the amount of runoff reaching the pipe in cubic feet per second, a value to use for Manning's n, and a hydraulics calculator. The method for determining the runoff is explained earlier in this chapter, the value to use for Manning's n will be dictated by the responsible agency or can be taken from Table 8-2, and the use of the hydraulics calculator is described in Chap. 7. The hydraulics calculator gives a range of sizes and corresponding slopes that can be used. The choice of size and slope is made based on (1) the criteria of the responsible agency, (2) the criteria affecting the design of the profile as described earlier, and (3) the cost of material and trenching. Keep in mind when selecting sizes that as the network progresses downstream, the pipe sizes must never get smaller even though the hydraulics of a steeper slope permit a smaller pipe. Each downstream pipe must be as big or bigger than the last to ensure that any debris that may have entered the system can continue without causing a blockage.

Though providing for a single drainage basin is simple, providing for multiple basins served by a piping network is complicated. A Storm Drainage System Calculations form is included here as Fig. 8-14. Most agencies have a similar form or a variation of it. When filled out correctly, the pipe sizes and slopes and flow velocities are shown. Filling out the form must be coordinated with the design of the profile and may have to be done more than once to coordinate with other criteria.

Filling out the form is complicated, so an example will be used for illustration. Note that, in this example, the t_c is given as the time for the drop of rain to reach the storm water inlets, whereas the t_c is often the time for a drop of rain to reach the gutter. Normally the t_c will have additional flow time between where the drop of rain enters the gutter and where it enters the inlet.

A flow time in the gutter can be calculated with the equation

$$t = \frac{l}{60\,V} \tag{8-4}$$

Return Period _____   Date _____
Manning's *n* _____   Designed by _____
                                       Checked by _____

STORM DRAINAGE SYSTEM CALCULATIONS

for

1	2	3	4	5	6	7	8	9	10	11	12	13	14	15	16
Point of concentration	Runoff factor C	Time of concentration, min	Rainfall intensity I, in/h	Total tributary area A, acres	Q, cfs	Pipe diameter, in	Slope, ft/100 ft	Velocity, ft/s	Length, ft	Time, min	Invert elevation		Top of pipe elevation	Rim or TG elevation	Cover, ft (15)−(14)
											In	Out			

Fig. 8-14 Storm drainage calculations form.

TABLE 8-3 **Approximate Mean Velocity of Flow in Gutters (Asphalt or Concrete with 6-in Curb)**

Gutter Slope	Velocity, fps
0.001	1.0
0.002	1.4
0.004	1.9
0.006	2.4
0.008	2.8
0.010	3.1
0.015	3.8
0.020	4.4

where t = flow time, min

l = length, ft

V = velocity, fps

The velocity of the flow can be taken from Table 8-3.

Example 8-3

Determine sizes, slopes, and inverts of the storm sewer network shown in Fig. 8-15. The sizes of drainage basins, times of concentration, and coefficents of runoff are specified in Fig. 8-15. The agency criteria follows.

Minimum slope 0.004

Minimum pipe size is 12 in

Requirement of 0.5-ft drop at connections with a change of direction of 30° or more

Storm Drainage Systems Calculations form (Fig. 8-14)

IDF Chart (Fig. 8-1)

10-year return period storm

Manning's n = 0.015 for pipes 12 to 33 in; n = 0.013 for pipes 36 in or larger

Solution

1. Fill in column 1. Start with the point of concentration farthest from the outfall. List the next point of concentration on the next line. If there is more than one pipe emptying into the second point of concentration, skip a line on the form and list the other point of concentration upstream of the second point. On the next line, list the second point of concentration again. When all sources discharging into a particular point of concentration have been listed, skip a line and list that point of concentration followed on the next line by the next downstream point of concentration. Continue through the network until all points of concentration have been listed (Fig. 8–17).
2. Fill in columns 2, 3, and 5 for the catch basins only. There is no overland runoff entering the manholes directly. All runoff reaching the manholes does so through pipes.
3. Using the t_c given in fig. 8-15 and a 10-year return period, find the rainfall intensity at each catch basin from Fig. 8-1. Enter intensity in column 4.

4. The quantity of runoff (Q, column 6) is determined with the rational formula (Eq. 8-1). Calculate Q for each catch basin by multiplying the values in columns 2, 4, and 5. Enter the products in column 6.

5. Using Q for CB no. 1 and the value of n given (0.015), use a hydraulics calculator to select a pipe size and slope. The runoff reaching CB no. 1 is 0.79 cfs. The diameter of a pipe, as read from the hydraulics calculator, that will accommodate 0.79 cfs at the minimum slope of 0.004 is between 8 and 10 in. The slope that will accommodate the 0.79 cfs with the minimum pipe size of 12 in is 0.00065. When minimum slope is used, the pipe size is smaller than minimum. When minimum size is used, the slope is too flat. Therefore, the minimum size pipe and the minimum slope will be used. A 12-in diameter pipe at a slope of 0.004 will allow a flow of 1.95 cfs. From this information it can be seen that all pipes carrying 0.95 cfs or less must have a 12-in diameter. Fill in columns 7 to 9 for the catch basins on the line between the points of concentration. Notice that the slope is given in feet per 100 ft. The slope (column 8) will be taken from the profile. Slopes are given arbitrarily for this example.

6. The lengths of the pipes are measured from the plans. In this example the lengths can be read from Fig. 8-15. Put the lengths of all the pipes into column 10.

7. Column 11 is used for the amount of time it takes for the runoff to flow through the pipe between the points of concentration in column 1. That time is calculated using Eq. 8-4 below.

$$t = \frac{l}{60\,V} \tag{8-4}$$

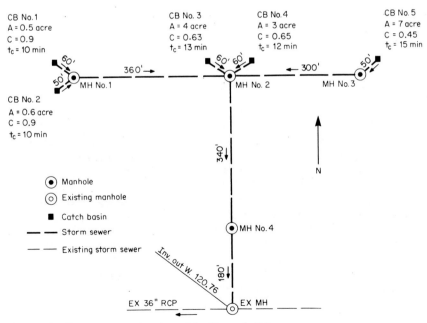

Fig. 8-15 Storm sewer network used for Example 8-3.

For the pipe between catch basin no. 1 and manhole no. 1

$$t = \frac{60 \text{ ft}}{60 \text{ s/min} \times 3.5 \text{ ft/s}} = 0.3 \text{ min}$$

Put the 0.3 min in column 11. Go through the same procedure for all the catch basins.

8. Enter the values of C and A (the total tributary area) for each manhole. At manhole no. 3, there is only one pipe entering, and the values of C and A are the same as at the contributing catch basin. When more than one pipe enters a manhole, a weighted average is used for the value of C.

From	A		C
CB no. 1	0.5 acres	$\times$	0.9 = 0.45
CB no. 2	0.6 acres	$\times$	0.9 = 0.54
MH no. 1	1.1 acres		0.99

at MH no. 1 $C = \dfrac{0.99}{1.10} = 0.9$

From	A		C
CB no. 3	4.0 acres	$\times$	0.63 = 2.52
CB no. 4	3.0 acres	$\times$	0.65 = 1.95
MH no. 1	1.1 acres	$\times$	0.90 = 0.99
MH no. 3	7.0 acres	$\times$	0.45 = 3.15
	15.1 acres		8.61

at MH no. 2, no. 4 and EX MH $C = \dfrac{8.61}{15.10} = 0.57$

The value of C thus derived should be entered on the form for each manhole but only where that manhole is at the upstream end of a pipe. The value of C will be entered only once for each manhole.

9. Next, determine the longest t_c required for the runoff to reach the manhole farthest from the outfall. The t_c at CB no. 1 is 10 min. The flow time from CB no. 1 to MH no. 1 is 0.3 min. The t_c at CB no. 2 is 10 min. The flow time from CB no. 2 to MH no. 1 is 0.2 min. The total t_c through CB no. 1 is 10.3 min. The total t_c through CB no. 2 is 10.2 min. Therefore, the longest t_c at MH no. 1 is 10.3 min. Enter 10.3 in column 3 opposite the third place in column 1 where MH no. 1 is listed. Using 10.3 min and the 10-year return period, obtain the value for intensity from Fig. 8-1 and enter the value in column 4. Complete columns 5 to 11 as previously described for MH nos. 2 and 4 and the existing MH.

10. Proceed by filling in the information for MH no. 3 and then for MH no. 2. The amount of flow being picked up at CB no. 5 exceeds the capacity of minimum conditions. There is a range of sizes and corresponding slopes from which to choose. The choice should be based on the factors discussed earlier in the section on profile design. The slopes used in this example are arbitrary.

The t_c at MH no. 2 must correspond to the single longest amount of time necessary for runoff to reach that manhole.

From	t_c + flow time		t_c to MH no. 2
MH no. 1	10.3 + 1.70	=	12.0 min
CB no. 3	13.0 + 0.20	=	13.2 min
CB no. 4	12.0 + 0.30	=	12.3 min
MH no. 3	15.2 + 1.40	=	16.6 min

As can be seen by inspection, the t_c from MH no. 3 is the longest. Therefore, 16.6 min is used to obtain the intensity and calculate the Q leaving MH no. 2. Making sense of the reasons for using this complex method requires an understanding of hydrologic concepts beyond the scope of this handbook.

11. Now the invert elevations can be set. The exact invert elevation of the outfall should be available from survey notes. When sewers are connected, the inside tops of the pipes are matched—not the inverts. Where there is a change of pipe sizes, there is also a change of invert elevations. A drop is also required where there is a change of direction.

    Starting at the outfall, work up the page. First, add to the outfall invert in column 13 the difference between the diameter of the outfall pipe and the incoming pipe.

$$36 \text{ in} - 18 \text{ in} = 18 \text{ in} = 1.5 \text{ ft}$$
$$120.76 \text{ ft} + 1.5 \text{ ft} = 122.26 \text{ ft}$$

There is a drop requirement of 0.5 ft here as the flow will change direction 90°. However, the difference in diameter exceeds the drop requirement, so the drop requirement is met and need not be added again. Now, enter this invert, 122.26, in column 12.

12. To calculate the invert at the upstream end of the pipe, multiply the length of the pipe (column 10) times the slope (column 8), remembering to convert to feet per foot, and add the product to the invert in column 12 across from the next upstream point of concentration.

$$180 \text{ ft} \times 0.014 \text{ ft} = 2.52 \text{ ft}$$
$$122.26 \text{ ft} + 2.52 \text{ ft} = 124.78 \text{ ft}$$

Put 124.78 in column 13 on the next line up opposite MH no. 4. The invert elevation into MH no. 4 equals the invert elevation going out. Multiply the length of the pipe from MH no. 4 to MH no. 2 times the slope for that section.

$$340 \text{ ft} \times 0.015 = 5.1 \text{ ft}$$

Add 5.1 ft to the elevation of the invert into MH no. 4.

$$124.78 \text{ ft} + 5.10 \text{ ft} = 129.88 \text{ ft}$$

129.88 is the invert elevation out of MH no. 2. Write 129.88 opposite all the listings for MH no. 2 in column 13.

13. The pipe entering MH no. 2 from the east is a 15-in-diameter pipe. The difference of pipe sizes is

$$18 \text{ in} - 15 \text{ in} = 3 \text{ in} = 0.25 \text{ ft}$$

Therefore, the invert must be at least 0.25 ft above the invert out of MH no. 2.

The agency requires a 0.5 ft difference when there is a change in the direction of flow which exceeds 30°.

$$0.5 \text{ ft} > 0.25 \text{ ft}$$

Add 0.5 ft to the invert out of MH no. 2 to obtain the invert into the manhole with the 15-in line.

$$129.88 \text{ ft} + 0.5 \text{ ft} = 130.38 \text{ ft}$$

Going through the same procedure produces the same invert in elevation for the 12-in line entering from the west.

14. The laterals entering MH no. 2 from the north (Fig. 8-16) will not fit into the manhole at the same elevation as the pipes entering from east and west. Therefore, 1.5 ft was added to the elevation of the inverts of the east and west lines to obtain the invert elevations of the north-entering laterals. This gives the northern laterals clearance vertically.

15. Continue up the page until an invert has been set for both ends of all pipes (Fig. 8-17).

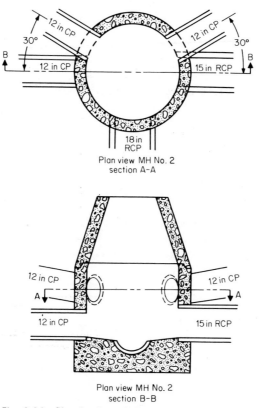

Plan view MH No. 2
section A-A

Plan view MH No. 2
section B-B

Fig. 8-16 Sketch of manhole no. 2 to check the fit of the pipe.

Return Period 10 yr _____ 10 yr _____   Date 1-31-83 _____ 1-31-83 _____

Manning's n _____ .015 _____   Designed by _____ L.B. _____

                                                Checked by _____ B.C. _____

STORM DRAINAGE SYSTEM CALCULATIONS
for
Example 8-3

1	2	3	4	5	6	7	8	9	10	11	12	13	14	15	16
											Invert elevation				
Point of concentration	Runoff factor C	Time of concentration, min	Rainfall intensity I, in/h	Total tributary area A, acres	Q, cfs	Pipe diameter, in	Slope, ft/100 ft	Velocity, ft/s	Length, ft	Time, min	In	Out	Top of pipe elevation	Rim or TG elevation	Cover, ft (15)−(14)
CB#1	0.9	10	1.75	0.5	0.79	12	.4	3.5	60	0.3		132.52			
MH#1											132.32	131.82			
CB#2	0.9	10	1.75	0.6	0.95	12	.4	3.5	50	0.2		132.56			
MH#1											132.32	131.82			
MH#1	0.9	10.3	1.70	1.1	1.68	12	.4	3.5	360	1.70		131.82			
MH#2											130.38	129.88			
CB#3	0.63	13	1.50	4.0	3.78	12	1.5	4.8	60	0.2		132.78			
MH#2											131.88	129.88			
CB#4	0.65	12	1.60	3.0	3.12	12	1.0	4.0	60	0.3		132.48			
MH#2											131.88	129.88			
CB#5	0.45	15	1.35	7.0	4.25	12	1.9	5.4	50	0.2		133.63			
MH#3	0.45	15.2	1.35	7.0	4.25	15	0.6	3.6	300	1.4	132.68	132.18			
MH#2											130.38	129.88			
MH#2	0.57	16.6	1.30	15.1	11.19	18	1.5	6.4	340	.89		129.88			
MH#4	0.57	17.5	1.25	15.1	10.76	18	1.4	6.2	180	.48	124.78	124.78			
EX MH	0.57	18.0	1.20	15.1	10.32						122.26	120.76			

Fig. 8-17 Storm drainage calculations form filled out.

Further information can be added to the form as needed. The difference between the invert and the top of the pipe for the various pipe sizes is available from the manufacturer. When the calculation of the profile is complete, critical points can be checked. When the responsible agency calls for criteria involving the hydraulic grade line and/or top-of-curb elevations, that information can be entered in columns 15 and 16.

The *hydraulic grade line* (HGL) is the line to which the water level will rise in a vertical tube above a pipe under pressure (Fig. 8-18). Ordinarily, storm sewers are designed for gravity flow and are not under pressure; however, where the outfall and/or storm water inlet is submerged, the HGL extends from the water surface over the outfall or inlet. When the pipe profile is in a sag vertical curve, the HGL extends from the inside top of the pipe in the manhole or storm water inlet at one end of the pipe to the inside top of the pipe in the manhole or inlet at the other end.

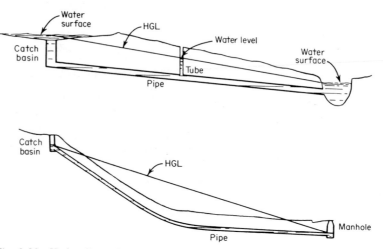

Fig. 8-18   Hydraulic grade line (HGL).

Example 8-4

Calculate the amount of cover over the surface low point at sta 8+78 in Fig. 8-19. The wall thickness of 24-in-diameter RCP is 0.30 ft.

Solution

1. Calculate the invert elevation at the critical point.

$$100 \text{ ft} + 0.004 \, [(8+78) - (8+20)] = 100.23 \text{ ft}$$

2. Add pipe diameter and wall thickness to get the top-of-pipe elevation.

$$100.23 \text{ ft} + 2.00 \text{ ft} + 0.30 \text{ ft} = 102.53 \text{ ft}$$

3. Subtract the surface elevation from the top-of-pipe elevation.

$$105.20 \text{ ft} - 102.53 \text{ ft} = 2.67\text{-ft cover}$$

Example 8-5

Calculate the amount of clearance over the top of the water main at sta 10+ 23 in Fig. 8-19. The wall thickness of 24-in-diameter RCP is 0.30 ft.

Solution

1. Calculate the invert elevation at the critical point.

$$100.96 \text{ ft} - 0.004 \ [(10+60) - (10+23)] = 100.81 \text{ ft}$$

2. Subtract wall thickness.

$$100.81 \text{ ft} - 0.30 \text{ ft} = 100.51 \text{ ft}$$

3. Subtract top of pipe elevation.

$$100.51 \text{ ft} - 98.68 \text{ ft} = 1.83 \text{ ft of clearance}$$

Technique for Shallow Sewers

When the site is nearly flat and the available outfalls are shallow, a different approach to designing the profile should be taken. When the horizontal layout is complete on the project master plan, the existing invert elevations should be marked in pencil. By starting at the outfall invert and applying the minimum allowable slope to the network of pipes, the sewers can be set at their deepest

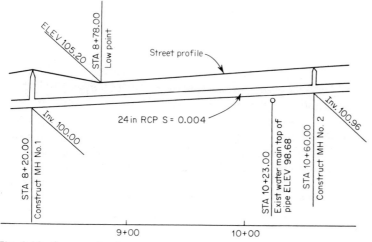

Fig. 8-19 Sewer main clearance.

possible location. The minimum slope is usually dictated by the agency and is based on the criterion that a minimum velocity of 2 to 2.5 fps is necessary to assure sufficient scouring of the line. Determine the invert elevations this way, and write them on the master plan in pencil.

The size of the pipes is not important at this stage except that when the connecting main is at minimum slope, the required diameter must not exceed the diameter of the outfall conduit. When the connecting pipe at minimum slope is larger than the outfall, its slope must be made steeper to accommodate the flow in the smaller pipe. The required diameter, in this case, is based on the total runoff Q_R that will be put into that outfall.

Estimate a value for C and a time of concentration. Use a hydraulics calculator to determine the required slope of the incoming pipe. Go through the same procedure with the sanitary sewer. Then calculate the clearances at crossings, and verify that there is enough clearance or enough flexibility in one of the systems to provide the clearance. It may be necessary to determine the pipe size based on the minimum slope at this time. If crossings cannot be made to clear, another layout should be tried.

Existing utilities that are not dependent on gravity flow can be relocated to clear the new sewers. However, relocating existing lines should be avoided whenever possible. When the site is too shallow to accommodate the storm system through the use of conventional methods, some alternatives that could be considered with respect to cost are: import fill to raise the site; use small parallel sewer networks; use an outfall that is deep enough though it is not adjacent to the site; provide a retention pond or a percolation pond.

A *percolation pond* is a reservoir constructed to hold water until it can seep into the ground. It is usually used to recharge the groundwater reservoir to provide for future water needs and to protect against subsidence of the ground caused by excessive withdrawals of groundwater by wells. But in this case, the percolation pond becomes the outfall.

Outfalls

When the outfall is a river, stream, or channel, there will be a flood control district or other public agency with jurisdiction over any discharges into it. Usually an encroachment and/or construction permit is required. The agency may have its own specifications and standard plans that must be adhered to. Discharge into a natural waterway may require meeting concerns of a fish and game department or the Environmental Protection Agency as well. Be aware that failure to get the appropriate permits from some obscure agency can shut down construction. Do not be afraid to ask a spokesperson for one agency if he or she knows of other agencies that might have jurisdiction.

When a site is an otherwise unimproved area, there may not be any existing outfalls available. When this is the case, a temporary outfall will sometimes be allowed by use of a bubbler (Fig. 8-20). Bubblers serve the reverse function of a storm water inlet. An inlet collects water from the surface and puts it into an

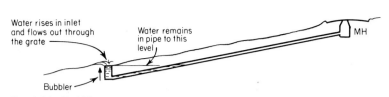

Fig. 8-20 Bubbler.

underground piping system. A *bubbler* is a storm water inlet that takes water from an underground piping system and puts it onto the surface.

The bubbler is installed at the end of the storm sewer system. Runoff reaching the end of the storm system fills the bubbler and overflows through the grate thereby becoming overland flow. The top-of-grate elevation of the bubbler must be below the invert of the next upstream manhole or storm water inlet. Water will remain in the system wherever the elevation is below the top-of-grate elevation of the bubbler. Because of this, some jurisdictions will not allow bubblers. A dry well can be built around the bubbler and drain holes placed at the bottom in its sides to drain the line.

SUBTERRANEAN WATER

Subterranean water can sometimes be a problem. The soils report may address this, but often the problem first becomes apparent during construction. Excessive groundwater can make construction of the improvements impossible, cause damage to building foundations, and greatly shorten the life of roads.

The Underground Ditch

One way of dealing with subterranean water is by constructing an underground ditch (French drain). A trench is dug to sufficient depth to protect the improvements from the flow of underground water. This task could entail encircling the improvements or simply constructing a drainage trench across a small, seasonal underground stream. A layer of permeable rock is laid in the bottom of the trench, perforated pipe is installed with the holes down, and then the trench is filled with permeable rock (Fig. 8-21). The subterranean water flows into the

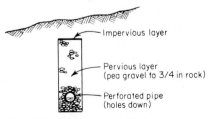

Fig. 8-21 Underground ditch.

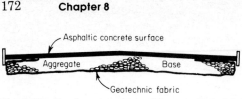

Fig. 8-22   Road cross section with geotechnic fabric.

trench, is drawn into the pipe, and is carried off. The perforated pipe must be connected to a storm sewer system or other outfall.

High Water Table

A high water table cannot be dealt with by installing a trench and perforated pipe; however, if not dealt with, it can cause a breakup of the roadbed in a short time. The problem comes as a result of the traffic loads. As traffic moves over the roadbed, a pumping action is created. The saturated subgrade is pumped into the baserock section of the road, destroying its continuity and structural qualities. To prevent this, a fabric membrane can be wrapped around the entire baserock layer (Fig. 8-22), separating it from the subgrade and subterranean water. This will ensure its continuity.

REFERENCES

Brater, E. F., and King, Horace: *Handbook of Hydraulics,* McGraw-Hill Book Co., New York, 1976.

County of Santa Clara: *Drainage Manual,* Santa Clara, CA, 1966.

Linsley, R. K., and Franzini, J. B.: *Water Resources Engineering,* 2d ed., McGraw-Hill Book Co., New York, 1972.

Metcalf & Eddy, Inc.: *Wastewater Engineering: Collection, Treatment, Disposal,* McGraw-Hill Book Co., New York, 1972.

State of California Division of Highways, *California Culvert Practices,* 2d ed., Sacramento, CA.

Viessman, Warren, Jr., Harhaugh, T. E., and Knapp, J. W.: *Introduction to Hydrology,* Intext Educational Publishers, New York, 1972.

Chapter Nine

Water Supply Lines

Of the various aspects of land development, the design of water supply lines may be the easiest. This is primarily because water supply lines are force mains (pressure lines). They are not dependent on gravity to flow, so they can be designed to go over or under other underground facilities without significant loss of water pressure or velocity. Their horizontal and vertical placement is thus dependent only on convenience, protection from crushing if within a traveled way, and protection from freezing in cold climates.

Though this chapter addresses water supply lines, the information generally holds true for other types of force mains as well.

WATER DEMAND

The size of the demand for water depends on climate, distribution of land use, cost of water, availability of private sources of water, and cultural attitudes. This fact is illustrated in Table 7-1. Notice that the consumption rate is shown as 50 gallons per day per capita (gpd/cap) in Little Rock, Arkansas, and 410 gpd/cap in Las Vegas, Nevada. The demand also varies throughout the day and throughout the year (Fig. 9-1).

Industrial

Some industries have a high demand for water. If you are designing a water supply system from a public water supply for an industrial park, this must be taken into consideration. If the user industries are known, obtain expected consumption rates from them. The water consumption rates for some industries are shown in Table 9-1.

Nonindustrial

Consumption rates for various nonindustrial establishments are shown in Table 9-2. An increasing concern for water conservation may result in appliances which use less water than indicated here. Obtain from the architect expected water demand when designing waterlines for high-demand buildings such as hotels and apartment houses.

A master plan which takes into account expected future growth should be available at the water supply agency. That agency may provide and install all the water supply lines, or it may be necessary for construction plans of the water supply lines to be provided with other improvements. In either case, the water agency will dictate the size and types of waterlines required.

Fire Protection

A major factor in determining pipe sizes and water pressures is provision for fire protection. A minimum of a 6-in waterline should be used to serve residential sites. In high-value districts use 8- or 10-in lines.

The waterlines for fire protection can be incorporated with the domestic sup-

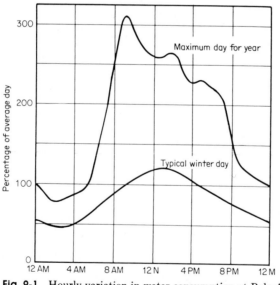

Fig. 9-1   Hourly variation in water consumption at Palo Alto, California. *(From Lindsay and Franzini, p. 430.)*

ply lines, or separate systems can be installed. When they are incorporated, fire protection demands draw from the domestic needs in an emergency.

THE PIPING NETWORK

The water company or agency may dictate the size, location, and types of pipes to be used. The sizing is based on fire protection requirements and expected consumption. There may be a standard location for waterlines such as 6 ft off the face of the curb or 2 ft behind the property line.

Waterlines that will be supplying drinking water must be protected from infiltration. This is partially accomplished with maintenance of water pressure within the system. For one-and two-story residential buildings in flat terrain, 45 pounds per square inch (psi) pressure is minimum. For water supply lines in steep terrain, 60 to 75 psi is recommended throughout the system. The pressure in water supply lines is usually provided by locating the water source on a hill or in tanks above the system, but water pressure can also be supplied by a pumping system. If the project site is at an elevation above surrounding terrain, check if the pressure will be sufficient for the project. Water supply lines should

TABLE 9-1 Water Consumption in Representative Industries*

Process	Consumption
Cannery:	
Green beans, gal/ton	20,000
Peaches and pears, gal/ton	5,300
Other fruits and vegetables, gal/ton	2,000–10,000
Chemical industries:	
Ammonia, gal/ton	37,500
Carbon dioxide, gal/ton	24,500
Gasoline, gal/1000 gal	7,000–34,000
Lactose, gal/ton	235,000
Sulfur, gal/ton	3,000
Food and beverage industries:	
Beer, gal/1000 gal	15,000
Bread, gal/ton	600–1,200
Meat packing, gal/ton live weight	5,000
Milk products, gal/ton	4,000–5,000
Whiskey, gal/1000 gal	80,000
Pulp and paper	
Pulp, gal/ton	82,000–230,000
Paper, gal/ton	47,000
Textiles	
Bleaching, gal/ton cotton	72,000–96,000
Dyeing, gal/ton cotton	9,500–19,000

*From Metcalf & Eddy, Inc., p. 32.

TABLE 9-2 Estimated Water Consumption at Different Types of Establishments*

Type of Establishment	Flow, GPD/ Person or Unit
Dwelling units, residential	
Private dwellings on individual wells or metered supply	50–75
Apartment houses on individual wells	75–100
Private dwellings on public water supply, unmetered	100–200
Apartment houses on public water supply, unmetered	100–200
Subdivision dwelling on individual well, or metered supply, per bedroom	150
Subdivision dwelling on public water supply, unmetered, per bedroom	200
Dwelling units, treatment	
Hotels	50–100
Boarding houses	50
Lodging houses and tourist homes	40
Motels, without kitchens, per unit	100–150
Camps	
Pioneer type	25
Children's, central toilet and bath	40–50
Day, no meals	15
Luxury, private bath	75–100
Labor	35–50
Trailer with private toilet and bath, per unit (2½ persons)†	125–150
Restaurants (including toilet):	
Average	7–10
Kitchen wastes only	2½–3
Short order	4
Short order, paper service	1–2
Bars and cocktail lounges	2
Average type, per seat	35
Average type, 24-h, per seat	50
Tavern, per seat	20
Service area, per counter seat (toll road)	350
Service area, per table seat (toll road)	150
Institutions	
Average type	75–125
Hospitals	150–250
Schools	
Day, with cafeteria or lunch room	10–15
Day, with cafeteria and showers	15–20
Boarding	75
Theaters	
Indoor, per seat, two showings per day	3
Outdoor, including food stand, per car (3⅓ persons)	3–5
Automobile service stations	
Per vehicle served	10
Per set of pumps	500
Stores	
First 25-ft frontage	450
Each additional 25-ft frontage	400
Country clubs	
Resident type	100
Transient type, serving meals	17–25
Offices	10–15

TABLE 9-2 **Estimated Water Consumption at Different Types of Establishments** *(continued)*

Type of Establishment	Flow, GPD/ Person or Unit
Factories, sanitary wastes, per shift	15–35
Self-service laundry, per machine	250–500
Bowling alleys, per alley	200
Swimming pools and beaches, toilet and shower	10–15
Picnic parks, with flush toilets	5–10
Fairgrounds (based on daily attendance)	1
Assembly halls, per seat	2
Airport, per passenger	2½

*From Metcalf & Eddy, Inc., pp. 29–30.

†Add 125 gal per trailer space for lawn sprinkling, car washing, leakage, etc. Note: Water under pressure, flush toilets, and wash basins are included, unless otherwise indicated. These figures are offered as a guide; they should not be used blindly. Add for any continuous flows and industrial usages. Figures are flows per capita per day, unless otherwise stated.

never be placed in a joint trench with storm and sanitary sewer lines. A minimum distance of 10 ft between waterlines and sewer lines should be maintained.

Pipes designed for high tensile strength as well as for crushing strength must be used for pressure mains. Cast-iron (CIP), cement-lined steel, asbestos cement (ACP), steel, plastic, and, for large lines, reinforced concrete (RCP) are the types of pipes produced for pressure systems. Plastic pipes designed specifically for forced systems are being used more and more frequently. Asbestos cement pipe is restricted in some areas and is generally being used less frequently for water supply lines due to increasing concern over the possible carcinogenic effect of asbestos.

Horizontal Layout

Whenever possible, water supply lines are laid out in a gridlike manner so that there are no dead ends. This is called "looping." The advantage of laying out the lines this way is that there are no dead ends in which water can stagnate, and if repairs are required, smaller areas will have the water supply cut off. Excessive demand put on the system by fire causes less head loss (pressure loss) in a gridlike system.

Sizing the piping system is usually done by the water company using the Hardy-Cross solution of successive approximations. Another technique is the nodal method. A description of these methods can be found in the *Handbook of Hydraulics*.[1]

[1]Brater, Ernest, and King, Horace: *Handbook of Hydraulics,* 6th ed., McGraw-Hill Book Co., New York, 1976, pp. 6-30 to 6-38.

Where the water pipe is to curve, deflections specified by the pipe manufacturer should be used. Where there are to be connections, tees and wyes should be used and described on the plans. Where there is to be a change of direction either horizontally or vertically, a bend should be used and described. Most pipe manufacturers have bends and elbows of 90°, 45°, 30°, 22½°, and 11¼° (Fig. 9-2). This limitation of available degrees of deflection for bends reduces flexibility of design.

Class equals crushing strength, lbs/lf (ASTM Test Method)	Pipe size Inside diameters, inches
1500	4, 5, 6
2400	4, 5, 6
3300	4, 5, 6

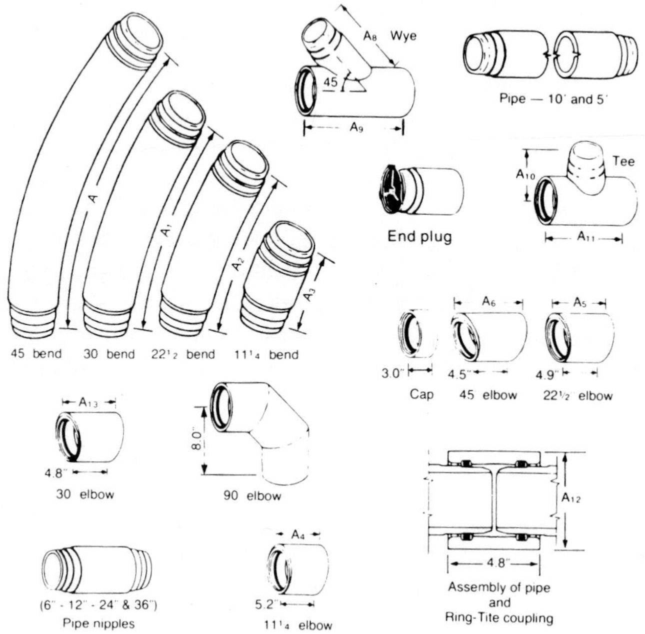

Dimensions, in Pipe size	A	A₁	A₂	A₃	A₄	A₅	A₆	A₈	A₉	A₁₀	A₁₁	A₁₂	A₁₃
4	28.3	18.9	14.1	7.1	6.5	7.4	10.0	10.0	14.0	7.0	11.3	5.9	8.3
5	37.7	25.1	18.9	9.4	6.7	7.9	10.9	11.4	16.0	7.5	12.3	7.0	8.8
6	37.7	25.1	18.9	9.4	6.9	8.3	11.7	12.6	17.3	8.0	13.3	8.0	9.4

Fig. 9-2 Bends and elbows. *(From Johns-Manville Transite pipe.)*

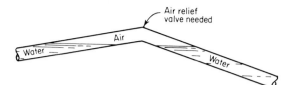

Fig. 9-3 Bubbles of air trapped in a piping system will float to a high point and can block flow.

The Profile

Available elbows and bends must be used to make necessary changes of direction in the profile as well. Wherever the waterline crosses other underground lines, a profile should be drawn and clearances verified. Inverts and slopes are calculated as they are with sewer lines; however, centers of pipes are matched rather than overts. Reducers, wyes, and tees are used for connections. A profile can have a positive or negative slope, but level sections should be limited to short distances. A slope of 0.005 is the minimum desirable to permit drainage of the lines.

Wherever the profile changes from positive to negative and at the ends of lines, an air-relief valve should be provided. Bubbles of air trapped in the system will float to a high point. This accumulation of air can block the passage of water and stop the system from working (Fig. 9-3). The air-relief valve allows trapped air to escape.

Where the profile changes from negative to positive, a drain or blow-off valve may be required so that the pipe can be drained for inspection and repair. This valve can also be used to flush the line to remove rust and debris. The change of slope for each type of bend is tabulated in Table 9-3.

Add the change of slope algebraically to the slope preceding the bend to determine the slope following the bend.

Example 9-1

Calculate the slopes for each of the sections of waterline shown in Figure 9-4. Use Table 9-3.

Solution

1. Calculate the algebraic sum of the slope A-B and the change of slope for a 45° bend.

$$
\begin{array}{ll}
-0.005 & \text{Slope } A\text{-}B \\
\underline{-1.000} & \underline{45° \text{ bend}} \\
-1.005 & \text{Slope } B\text{-}C
\end{array}
$$

Table 9-3 Bends

	Degree of deflection	Change of slope		Degree of deflection	Change of slope
	90°	+2.0000		90°	−2.0000
	45°	+1.0000		45°	−1.0000
	30°	+0.5774		30°	−0.5774
	22½°	+0.4142		22½°	−0.4142
	11¼°	+0.1989		11¼°	−0.1989

2. Continue in the same manner for the other sections.

$$
\begin{array}{ll}
-1.005 & \text{Slope } B\text{-}C \\
+1.000 & 45° \text{ bend} \\
\hline
-0.005 & \text{Slope } C\text{-}D
\end{array}
$$

$$
\begin{array}{ll}
-0.005 & \text{Slope } C\text{-}D \\
+0.414 & 22½° \text{ bend} \\
\hline
+0.409 & \text{Slope } D\text{-}E
\end{array}
$$

$$
\begin{array}{ll}
+0.409 & \text{Slope } D\text{-}E \\
-0.577 & 30° \text{ bend} \\
\hline
-0.168 & \text{Slope } E\text{-}F
\end{array}
$$

When drawing the waterline profile, remember that the horizontal and vertical scales are different, so a 45° bend will not result in a 45° angle on the profile.

Because the forced system must be designed around the gravity systems, the space for elbows, bends, wyes, and tees may be limited. If this is the case, it is

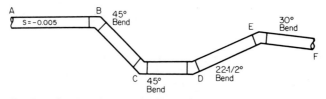

Fig. 9-4   Section of piping for Example 9-1.

important to get the manufacturer's specifications, to make a drawing using a natural scale, and to verify the clearances.

APPURTENANCES

There are a variety of valves and other appurtenances associated with force main systems. The purpose of air-relief, blow-off, and drain valves has been described. Some other valves you may encounter are check valves, pressure-relief valves, air-inlet valves, and pressure-regulating valves. Gate valves are used to regulate the flow in pipes and are located at many places in the system.

The system will also include fire hydrants, thrust blocks, and water meters which will be described briefly in this section.

Gate Valves

The need to stop the flow of water at various locations in the piping network is met with gate valves. These valves are placed on each side of intersections and should be located no more than a ¼ mi apart along the waterline. Their placement should be based on cutting off water to the least number of people when repairs or alterations are made. When waterlines are located in streets, they should be placed out of the traveled way as much as possible. Each valve is enclosed in a valve box with a cover. The cover is usually marked with the word "water" and is made to withstand traffic loads when located in the street. In most cases, the valve box has a diameter of 6 to 8 in, but large gate valves may have to be placed in manholes. An example of a gate valve is shown in Fig. 9-5.

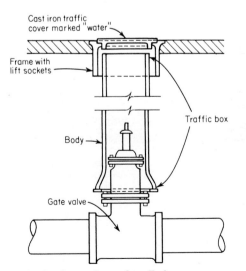

Fig. 9-5   Gate valve and traffic box.

Fire Hydrants

The locations of fire hydrants will be dictated by the fire department or another agency charged with public safety. Their type and placement will be based on what equipment is available to the fire department.

Typically there is one at every intersection so that hoses can be pulled in any direction. They should be placed no more than 500 ft apart to avoid excessive head loss in an emergency. A break-away spool at the groundline will prevent damage below ground in case of an accident. A gate valve should be installed where the pipe connects to the main (Fig. 9-6).

Thrust Blocks

A change in the velocity or direction of flow in a pipe causes a change in the direction and magnitude of the momentum (force = mass times velocity). To absorb the force of momentum and to anchor bends and tees, concrete thrust blocks are constructed (Fig. 9-7). The location and sizes of these thrust blocks will be described in standard plans and specifications or should be shown on a detail sheet. Where clearances for the force main must be checked, be sure to include the thrust blocks.

Fig. 9-6   Fire hydrant with gate valve.

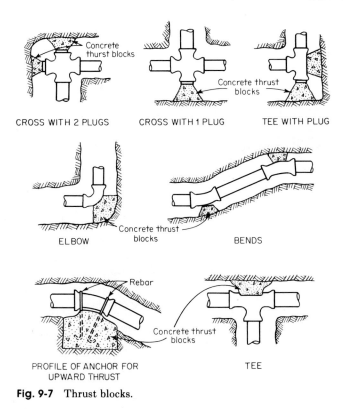

CROSS WITH 2 PLUGS   CROSS WITH 1 PLUG   TEE WITH PLUG

ELBOW   BENDS

PROFILE OF ANCHOR FOR
UPWARD THRUST   TEE

Fig. 9-7 Thrust blocks.

Laterals and Meters

Water supply laterals to single-family homes are usually ¾- to 1¼-in pipes. The connections are made with a tapping device called a "corporation cock." Flexible copper tubing or plastic pipe carries the water to the water meter. Connections for services larger than 2 in are made with tees and galvanized steel, plastic, or asbestos cement pipes.

The type of water meter and meter box should be specified by the water supply agency. Each lot may have a lateral, or there may be one lateral with a connection to two meters.

REFERENCES

Brater, Ernest F. and King, Horace: *Handbook of Hydraulics,* McGraw-Hill Book Co., New York, 1976.

Linsley, Ray K. and Franzini, Joseph B.: *Water-Resources Engineering,* McGraw-Hill Book Co., New York, 1972.

Viessman, Warren, Jr., Harbaugh, Terence E., and Knapp, John: *Introductions to Hydrology,* Intext Educational Publishers, New York, 1972.

Chapter Ten

The Finished Plans

The culmination of the engineering design will be the preparation of the finished plans. They should be a clear representation of the completed engineering design and the construction work to be done. The plans will represent your company and its engineering expertise. If the drawings are sloppy, hard to read, or amateurish, people viewing the plans may expect that the engineering will be sloppy and amateurish as well.

Employment of highly skilled, experienced drafters is important to the overall success of the project. A drafter experienced in land development work will often recognize transposed numbers or other errors in time to have the engineer make corrections.

The approving agency or consulting firm may have specific requirements as to what must be included in a set of plans and how they are to be presented. If a check list is available, obtain one and use it. A check list is included as a guide at the end of this chapter as Fig. 10-6.

All the sheets of a set of plans should have:

1. A border and a title block. The title block should show the project name—tract number, address, or whatever information will quickly identify it and distinguish it from other projects.
2. The engineering consultant or consulting firms with their names, addresses, and telephone numbers.
3. The signatures and titles or license numbers of responsible design engineers and approving agents.
4. A sheet number with the total number of sheets (e.g., sheet 1 of 10).
5. The scale or scales used.
6. The date of completion and/or approval of the plans.

7. A revision block with space to identify what revision was made, by whom, and on what date.

Most established engineering firms have plan sheets on which much of the information listed above is printed. The plan sheets usually are either vellum, a high-grade tracing paper, or mylar, a polyester, filmlike material. Mylar can be purchased with a matte finish on one or both sides for ease of drawing. The vellum and mylar can be purchased in various size sheets or rolls.

The approving agency may require that plans be a standard size or be drawn on standard sheets. The client may want the same size sheet used for architectural, structural, and site plans.

When the plans are finished, prints are made and sent to the approving agencies for review. The agents examine and check the plans for completeness and compliance with their criteria. Changes and additions are marked on the plans or are listed. The amount of time this takes varies depending on the work load. When the changes and additions have been made, the revised plans are sent to the agencies for approval signatures. A set of the construction plans will be kept on hand at the public works department and/or approving agency. Some take the original drawings. Others require a reproducible copy. If the originals are to be relinquished, have good reproducible copies made for your files.

THE COVER SHEET (TITLE PAGE)

Each set of plans should include a cover sheet (Fig. 10-1). What is appropriate to include on a cover sheet will vary from situation to situation. Some of the possibilities will be described here:

1. A vicinity or location map should be included to show where the site is located. This map may be at the center of the cover sheet and take up most of the space, or it may be placed in a corner taking up an area no more than 4 in × 4 in. The map should show major streets, have a north arrow, and the site should be clearly delineated. It may or may not be drawn to scale.
2. A general plan showing the entire project to scale may be included to show the relative locations of streets and lots. The name of the streets and the numbers of the lots should be shown. Reference should be made on the general plan to which of the interior sheets of the plans show the plan and profile of each street. Easements should be shown.
3. A legend should be shown identifying the meaning of the various symbols used throughout the plans.
4. A basis of bearings used for the streets and lots. An example of the basis of bearings is:

"The bearing N 89°30'08" E of the center line of Main Street as shown upon that Record of Survey field in Book 24 of Maps, page 8, Shasta County Records, was used as the basis of bearing."

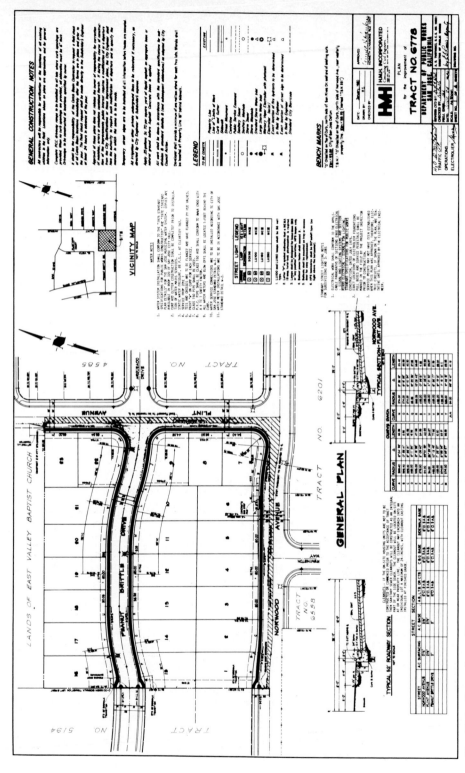

Fig. 10-1 Cover sheet. (*Courtesy of H.M.H., Inc., San Jose, CA.*)

5. The location and description of the bench mark should be shown. An example is:

   "An "X" chiseled in the top of curb at the curb return on the northwest corner of Main Street at Second Street. Bench mark elevation 103.36."

6. A table of contents or index of sheets is sometimes appropriate.
7. Construction notes may be included. For example, "All work must be done in accordance with the Standard Specification of the City of Springfield."
8. Various other details may be shown on the cover sheet.

PLAN AND PROFILE SHEETS

The instructions of how to build the project will be described with drawings and written explanations on the plan and profile sheets (Fig. 10-2). Using these sheets the surveyors will mark all the surface and subsurface improvements. Every point of change, whether a sanitary manhole or existing centerline, must be delineated and dimensioned so that the surveyors will be able to physically re-create the plans on the site. The surveyors locate significant points on the ground and mark those points with 2×2 wooden stakes called "hubs." A simple description of what the hub represents is written on a $\frac{1}{2} \times 2$ stake placed next to the hub. The various contractors then construct the improvements from the information on this stake.

The Plan View

Much of the information to be drawn on the plan view has been described throughout this book. All or a portion of a street or easement with accompanying utility lines will be shown. Reference to the sheet where plans for adjacent and/or connecting streets and utility lines are located should be placed at the connecting point, such as the street intersection. This may refer to another sheet on the same set of plans or, if the adjacent improvements are existing, to the tract or subdivision number. The street name and a north arrow should be included on each drawing.

The centerline (₵) of the street is placed in the center of the plan view space so that the north arrow will point either toward the top or right of the page. The centerline is drawn with straight courses and circular (highway) curves.[1]

All the new construction will be tied to the centerline reference line. The right-of-way lines for the streets should be shown, and the lot lines, lot numbers, and distances along lot frontages should be drawn along the right-of-way line. It is useful to have the lot lines referenced to the centerline. This way sewer and water laterals as well as driveways can be located and referenced. Utilities

[1] In some countries, spiral curves are used for streets and highways. Spiral curves are used for railroads in the United States.

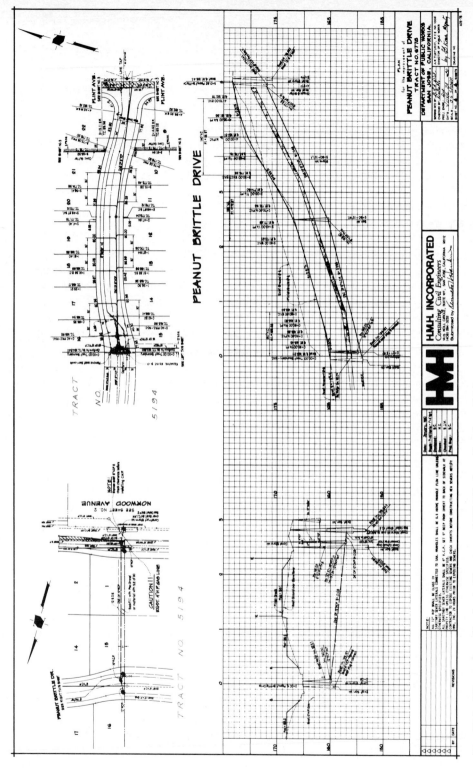

Fig. 10-2 Plan and profile sheet. *(Courtesy of H.M.H., Inc., San Jose, CA.)*

are referenced to the centerline so that survey crews can use the centerline stakes to locate manholes, water valves, and other facilities.

The layout of the storm and sanitary sewers is shown on the plan view. Manholes should be shown and numbered. This way if the same manhole is shown on more than one sheet of the plans, it will not be counted more than once. The mains should be labeled with the length and type of pipe. The sanitary laterals, catch basins with their laterals, and, in some jurisdictions, waterlines with laterals and water meters must all be shown. When there is an off-site utility line designed to go along an existing street or in an easement, it should be shown on the plan view and the profile. The street widths, distances between curbs, and dimensions to utility lines should be labeled at the ends of the street or wherever there is a change of location.

When preparing the plans, particular attention must be directed toward the edges and boundaries of improvements.

Wherever new streets connect with existing streets, a conform must be described and delineated on the plans. Where curbs are to meet, a note "meets existing curb" and an elevation followed by " $\pm$ " should be shown.

New conduits will connect with existing lines or will enter existing manholes. Where conduits are to be connected directly to the end of an existing main, a note "remove plug and connect" should be shown on the plan view. In some cases it will be necessary to remove a flushing inlet or clean out at the end of an existing sanitary sewer line. Where existing waterlines to be connected end in a blow-off valve, the valve will require removal. Where an existing manhole is to be entered with a new conduit, "break and enter" should be written on the plans at the manhole. Where sanitary laterals are to be connected to existing mains, reference to construction technique (e.g., "tap and saddle") must be noted.

It may be necessary to remove existing power poles and relocate other utility facilities. All these activities must be described so that their costs can be determined and construction progress can be properly coordinated.

The Profiles

A grid is provided to show the profiles. It should be stationed, and elevations should be shown at the edges. This facilitates plotting and reading. The horizontal scale will match the plan view, but the vertical scale is usually different to better illustrate vertical information. Unless the slope is steep, a vertical scale should be selected that will show the full length of the profile without running off the grid vertically. When otherwise expedient, a vertical scale one-tenth of the horizontal scale should be used. For example, if the horizontal scale is 1 in = 40 ft, use 1 in = 4 ft vertically. This way there is less likelihood of scaling an incorrect value when using more than one scale. Where slopes are steep, it may be necessary to break the profile at a match line and continue with a different elevation (Fig. 10-3). Where it has been necessary to use an equation in the plan view, that equation must be shown on the profile (Fig. 10-

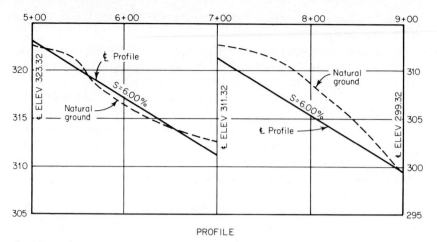

Fig. 10-3 Steep slopes may require that the profile be broken.

4). This is accomplished by restationing the profile from the next even grid line. The elevation must be the same on the stationing backward as on the stationing forward. Avoid locating any change of slope at an equation as the match will be less apparent and may cause confusion.

The existing natural groundline at the centerline must be drawn on and labeled. When the profile is not within a street right-of-way, show the proposed pad profile. Pertinent underground facilities must be shown and identified. If there are many existing and proposed utilities, it may be necessary to separate areas of profiles. All the existing and proposed utilities on one side of the street should be shown on one profile. The existing and proposed utilities on the other side of the street should be shown on another. This approach should be used

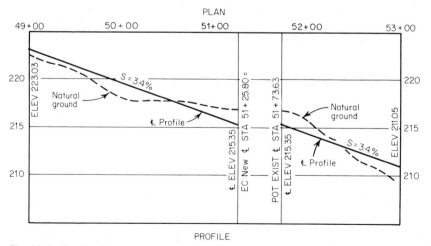

Fig. 10-4 Profile with equation.

only in extreme cases as conflicts and crossings will be less apparent and are more likely to be missed.

Show and identify street centerlines. The grades and vertical curve data must be shown. The stations and elevation of beginning and ends of vertical curves (BVC and EVC) must be shown and identified. The length of the curve, the station and elevation of the point of intersection (PI), and the grades must be shown as well. It will be necessary to give elevations on the profile of vertical curves at the midpoint and at intervals frequently enough for surveyors to mark the profile for construction of a smooth roadway. This distance may be at quarter points and/or eighth points, or some even interval such as 25 ft may work better. At the ends of the profile will be an equation with a connecting street or the tract boundary. A note to "conform to existing" may be appropriate.

The storm and sanitary profiles may be shown with a symbol, a single line, or a double line to indicate the top and bottom of the pipe. The sanitary sewer is shown with a single solid line and the storm sewer is shown with a single dashed line as in Fig. 10-2. The manholes are shown symbolically with slender triangles. If there is any question of fit, show the manhole to scale either on the plan and profile or in a detail. The manholes should be labeled such as "Construct sanitary M.H. #3 5 ft lt STA 3+23.56." The invert elevations should be labeled and identified such as "15 in ACP INV 221.53 thru, 12 in ACP in S. INV 221.78." Elevations on street and utility profiles should be labeled at the sheet match line.

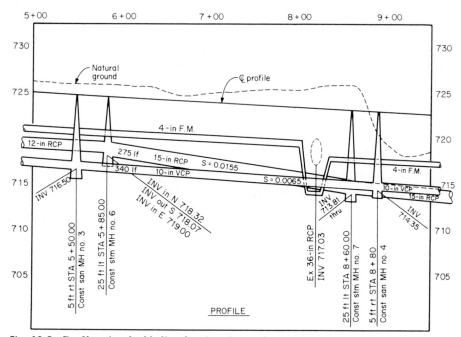

Fig. 10-5   Profile using double line drawings for conduits.

A FINISHED PLANS CHECK LIST

Cover Sheet

Title block
_____ Name and address of project
_____ Name and address of approving agency
_____ Names of approving agents with titles
_____ Names of approving departments
_____ Name, address, and phone number of consulting engineer
_____ Date
_____ Scale
_____Revision block w/date and initials
_____Sheet number and total sheets

A general plan
_____ Street names
_____ Lots
_____ Blocks
_____ Adjacent tract numbers
_____ Scale
_____ North arrow

A vicinity map
_____ Street names
_____ The site
_____ A north arrow
_____ Scale
_____Index of sheet's plan
_____Legend
_____Basis of bearings
_____Bench mark(s)
_____Details
_____Street structural cross section
_____Notes

Plan and Profile Sheets

Title block
_____ Name and address of project
_____ Name and address of approving agency
_____ Names and titles of approving agents
_____ Names of approving departments
_____ Name, address, and phone number of consulting engineer
_____ Date
_____ Scale
_____Revision block w/date and initials
_____Sheet number and total sheets
_____Stationing
_____Elevations
_____Street name(s)
_____Name of reference line(s)
_____North arrow(s)

Fig. 10-6 Finished plans check list.

_____Block numbers
_____Lot numbers
_____Reference to sheets showing adjacent areas
_____Center line stationing
_____Lot lines
_____ Stations
_____ Top of curb elevations
_____Face of curb data
_____Conforms
_____Barricades
_____Transitions
_____Signing and striping
_____Existing natural ground line

New and existing streets
_____ Center lines
_____ Right-of-way lines
_____ Face of curb lines
_____ Slopes
_____ Elevations

New and existing storm sewers
_____ Manholes
_____ Mains and laterals
_____   Lengths
_____   Size
_____   Type
_____   Slope
_____   Invert elevations
_____ Catch basins
_____   Type
_____   Size
_____ Ditches
_____   Type
_____   Slope
_____ Cross sections
_____ Outfall structures

New and existing sanitary sewers
_____ Manholes
_____ Mains and laterals
_____   Lengths
_____   Sizes
_____   Type
_____   Slope
_____   Invert elevations

New and existing water lines
_____ Mains and laterals
_____   Lengths
_____   Sizes
_____   Type
_____   Slopes

FIG. 10-6   (continued)

_____   Bends
_____   Elevations
_____   Water meters
_____   Fire hydrants
_____   Valves
      New and existing gas lines
_____   Size
_____   Type
_____   Valves
      New and existing electrical lines
_____   Size
_____   Type
_____   Power poles
_____   Transformers
      New and existing electroliers
_____   Conduit and conductors
_____   Junction boxes
      New and existing telephone lines
_____   Poles
_____   Junction boxes
_____   Manholes
      Notes

Fig. 10-6   (continued)

Drafting style can serve to clarify what might otherwise be confusing (Fig. 10-5). If there are several profiles in the same vertical space, different symbols can be used for each or the double-line drawing can be used with hidden lines representing places where one conduit is behind another. When the double-line approach is used, the symbol for a manhole should be removed where the conduit connects. Conduits behind manholes should be drawn as hidden lines. Existing conduits should be shown with lighter lines than proposed conduits.

When the drafting is complete, calculate the profiles from the finished drawings being careful to truncate elevation values beyond hundredths of a foot at grade breaks. This is a good check for drafting errors and ensures that values calculated will agree with those shown regardless of where the profile calculation is begun.

Finally, the check list should be consulted to be certain that everything has been done (see Fig. 10-6).

DETAIL DRAWINGS

There may be a need to include sheets of detail drawings. Where there are no standard plans and where the situation requires unusual or unique structures not standardized, the structures must be designed and drawings prepared. If there are many details necessary, it may be useful to have sheets designated such as "Storm Sewer Details" or "Water Facilities Details." A clear title such as "Sanitary Manhole 5 ft left of sta 50+20 on Main Street" should be provided. Drawings using different scales may be grouped together on the same sheet. When this is the case, each drawing should have the scale clearly labeled.

Chapter Eleven

The Construction Phase

Once the plans are complete and approvals and permits have been acquired, the project moves into the construction phase.

CONTRACTS AND SPECIFICATIONS

Engineers are often asked to write contracts and specifications for projects they have designed. Ordinarily standard contract forms are provided by the developer or are available from previous projects. Typically these forms have information to be filled in that will vary from job to job. Read the form being used and collect the necessary information. The kinds of information that may be needed are the:

Number of days until commencement of construction
Number of days until completion
Penalty levied for not meeting deadlines
Definition of extra work
Methods of payment
Responsibility for inspection
Responsibility for survey stakes
Procedures for dealing with discrepancies
Performance bond requirements
Liability and workman's compensation insurance requirements
Requirements for providing "equal opportunities"
Requirements for the condition and safety of the site
Requirements for dust and erosion control

The contracts may be nonspecific and say simply that the contractor has seen the job site and agrees to provide the labor, equipment, and materials necessary for construction and that the work will begin and be completed within a certain number of days. Attached to the contract will be a list of the quantities of the various items needed for construction. The descriptions may be nonspecific as "4 sanitary manholes," or may include exacting descriptions of the types of materials and construction methods to be used.

Specifications

When exacting descriptions of the types of materials and methods of construction are necessary, specifications must be written. Most public agencies have standard specifications in the form of a book that is available to the public for the price of printing and handling. The book is arranged in sections and subsections for easy access to needed information.

For jobs requiring specifications, refer to these standard specifications in general. All jobs have at least some situations that do not fit the standard plans and/or standard specifications. When this is the case, a clear description of materials and methods must be written. The engineer responsible for the design of the project and/or special structures must describe how construction is to be accomplished.

Quantities Takeoff

An important part of the contract is a list of the items to be built. The contract may state that the list is an estimate and that the contractor is responsible to build the project regardless of what is required. What this means is that the contractor must calculate his or her own estimate of the material needed and be satisfied with the list provided.

The exact length of the curb and gutter and the square footage of paving needed can be calculated from the plans. Particular attention must be given to the descriptions when there is more than one type of the same kind of item. For example, adjusting the grade of a manhole rim that must be raised will cost less than adjusting the rim of a manhole that must be lowered. Installation of a sanitary sewer main before paving is laid costs less than the installation of a sewer main when existing pavement must be removed and replaced. Catch basins with galleries cost more than standard catch basins.

Items dimensioned as linear feet should be precise to within a foot. Items dimensioned as square feet should be precise to within 1 ft^2 if the total is less than 100 ft^2—within 10 ft^2 if the total is greater than 100 ft^2. Earthwork quantities should be rounded to 10 yd^3. It may be necessary to convert square feet of paving or aggregate base to tons. The conversion factors are dependent on the asphalt mix and on the type of aggregate base being used, so these factors must be determined for each item.

Spread Sheet

Many developers—whether public or private—make use of a spread sheet (Fig. 11-1). The spread sheet lists the items and their quantities along one edge and the contractors bidding for the project along another edge. With each contractor a unit price and a total price are listed across from each item. The prices for all the items for each contractor are totaled. This allows an easy comparison of individual unit prices as well as totals.

Whenever possible, get a copy of the completed spread sheet. A file of spread sheets makes an ideal reference for estimating costs for similar projects.

CONSTRUCTION

When the project goes into construction, your responsibility is not over. Any work you have done incorrectly or incompletely and any design or specification that is not clear will come back to haunt you. If you have "done your home-

SPREAD SHEET								
Quantity	Description of item	Engineer's estimate		Contractor		Contractor		Contractor	
		Unit price	Total	Unit price	Total	Unit price	Total	Unit price	Total
		Total		Total		Total		Total	

Fig. 11-1 Spread sheet.

work"—been thorough in your research and single minded in resolving any uncertainty—you can enter the construction phase with confidence.

The Preconstruction Meeting

Often a preconstruction meeting is planned. Representatives of the developer, engineer, contractors, and utility companies meet—possibly on the site—and discuss how the work will progress and arrange coordination.

Questions may arise about conditions on the site or details on the plans. Review the plans, specifications, and quantities list before attending so that the information will be fresh in your mind. Be sure to take a set of plans and specifications with you. Do not rely on others to supply them. If you are asked a question you are not prepared to answer, offer to get the answer as soon as possible.

Construction Troubleshooting

Occasionally unanticipated situations become apparent during construction. Ancient utility lines are uncovered, a vein of hard rock makes conventional trenching techniques impractical, or neighbors think the work is encroaching on their land. When this happens, the people involved will look to the engineer for explanations and direction.

This is always an emotionally charged situation. It is imperative that your appearance be one of calm self-confidence. Solution to the problem will be obscured when tempers flare and fears are exaggerated. Often it is difficult to get a clear understanding of the problem until people are calm.

Initially there will be a phone call reporting that there is a problem and asking you to go to the site. Get as much information as possible. Ask the caller to be specific. The problem may be solved more quickly if you do not go to the site. You will have greater resources in the form of maps, plans, computers, and other engineers in your office than in the field. In the process of explaining the problem in a clear way, the caller may realize the solution immediately or with a little additional information from you.

When changes are made during construction, it is important that they are marked on the as-built plans and that all affected parties are informed.

Appendix A

Conversion Table

Lengths

1 inch (in)   25.4 millimeter (mm)
39.37 inches   1 meter (m)
12 inches = 1 foot (ft)
3 feet = 1 yard
1 mile = 5280 feet   1.609 kilometers (km)
1 chain (surveyor's) = 100 feet
1 link (surveyor's) = 1 foot
1 chain (Gunter's) = 66 feet = 4 rods
1 link (Gunter's) = 0.66 feet
1 rod = 16.5 feet

Area

1 square inch (in^2)   645 square millimeters (mm^2)
10.76 square feet (ft^2)   1 square meter (m^2)
1 square yard = 9 square feet
1 acre = 43,560 square feet   0.4047 hectare (ha)
2.47 acres   100 are = 1 hectare
100,000 square (Gunter's) links = 160
square rods
10 square (Gunter's) chain   4046.87 square meters
1 square (Gunter's) chain = 0.1 acre
1 section = 1 square mile = 640 acres

Volume

35.28 cubic feet (ft^3)   1 cubic meter
1 acre foot = 43,560 cubic feet
1 U.S. wet gallon   0.833 imperial gallons = 3.785 liters
1 cubic foot = 7.48 gallons (gal)
1 cubic yard = 27 cubic feet

Discharges

1 cubic foot per second (cfs) = 0.646
million gallons per day (million gpd or
mgd)   0.0283 cubic meters per second (m^3/s)
35.3 cubic feet per second (cfs)   1 cubic meter per second

Weight

1 pound (lb)   454 grams (g)
1 U.S. ton = 2000 pounds
1 long ton (Great Britain) = 2240 pounds   1016 kilograms (kg)
62.4 pounds per 1 cubic foot of water
1 gal water = 8.33 pounds
1 U.S. sack of cement = 94 pounds
1 U.K. sack of cement   50 kilograms (kg)
1 Canadian sack of cement = 87.5 pounds

Appendix B

Helpful Trigonometry

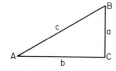

sine, sin of an angle = side opposite divided by hypotenuse

$$\sin A = \frac{a}{c}$$

$$\sin B = \frac{b}{c}$$

cosine, cos of an angle = side adjacent divided by hypotenuse

$$\cos A = \frac{b}{c}$$

$$\cos B = \frac{a}{c}$$

tangent, tan of an angle = side opposite divided by side adjacent

$$\tan A = \frac{a}{b}$$

$$\tan B = \frac{b}{a}$$

Law of sines

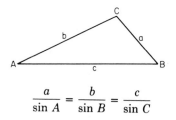

$$\frac{a}{\sin A} = \frac{b}{\sin B} = \frac{c}{\sin C}$$

Appendix C

Helpful Geometry

Circle

circumference $= 2\pi r$
area $= \pi r^2$

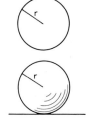

Sphere

surface area $= 4\pi r^2$
volume $= \frac{4}{3}\pi r^3$

Triangle

area $= \frac{1}{2} bh$

Trapezoid

area $= \dfrac{b_1 + b_2}{2} h$

Circular Cylinder

volume $= \pi r^2 l$

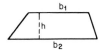

Right Circular Cone

total surface area $= \pi rl + \pi r^2$
volume $= \frac{1}{3}(\pi r^2 h)$

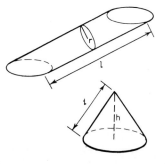

Glossary

A

AASHTO, The American Association of State Highway and Transportation Officials, Washington, DC.

AB, aggregate base.

A.B., anchor bolt. A bolt with the threaded part projecting from the concrete to secure framing or other structural members.

AC, asphaltic concrete. Material used for paving streets, parking lots, and sidewalks. Composed of bituminous petroleum products mixed with aggregate.

ACP, asbestos cement pipe. Formerly used extensively for water supply mains. Also used for sewer lines.

adverse grade, refers to a slope, particularly of a sewer where sewer slope is positive (up) where the groundline profile over the sewer is negative (down).

ADT, abbreviation for average daily traffic. The number of cars passing a particular point on an average day.

aerial, relating to or occurring in the air. For example, aerial power lines are mounted on poles, and aerial photographs are taken from an airplane.

agency, political body responsible for approval of a particular aspect of the design, i.e., city, county, flood control district, sanitation district.

aggregate, clean broken rock used for the preparation of concrete, asphaltic paving, and as base material for structures. The material is classified according to size between sand and 3 in.

annexation, legal procedure by which a political area such as a city can add more territory.

appurtenance, addition or accessory to something else.

APWA, American Public Works Association, 1313 East Sixtieth Street, Chicago, IL 60637.

ASB, aggregate subbase. Specified material to be placed below the foundation of a structure.

ASCE, American Society of Civil Engineers, 345 East 47th Street, New York, NY 10017-2398.

ASTM, American Society for Testing and Materials, 1916 Race Street, Philadelphia, PA 19103.

axis of rotation (Fig. 6-20), point about which the cross slope of a street is rotated.

B

backflow prevention device, check valve to prevent sewage from backing up into the plumbing facilities within a building if the downstream sewerage fails to function properly.

balance, term used to describe the situation when the volume of required earthwork excavation equals the volume of required earthwork fill.

base map, plan showing only that information basic to several aspects of the design (actually not a map). Copies of the base map are made and information needed for various aspects is added to separate copies thereby saving repeated drafting of the same information.

bench, horizontal shelf formed in a cut or fill slope. The bench reduces the risk of landslides and provides space to collect drainage for safe removal.

bench mark, vertical reference point.

BM, bench mark.

bend (Fig. 9-2), a conduit formed with a curve of specified deflection.

BSL, building setback line.

bulkhead, retaining wall.

bulking factor, number expressing the amount of increase in volume upon excavation of densely packed earth.

C

CAD, computer-aided drafting.

catch basin (Fig. 8-7*b*), storm water inlet, usually located in the curb and gutter of a road.

catch point (Fig. 5-9), place where a cut slope or a fill slope meets natural ground.

cfs, cubic feet per second.

cfm, cubic feet per minute.

check value, device which allows fluid to flow in only one direction.

chord, nontangent line segment which cuts across a circle but does not go through the center of it.

CIP, cast-iron pipe. Used where compressive strength is needed because of shallowness or where tensile strength is needed for pressure lines.

CIPP, cast-in-place pipe. Used where very large concrete pipe is needed.

CMP, corrugated metal pipe. Usually used for culverts and storm water outfalls. When CMP is used, it should be accompanied by required gauge.

CO (Fig. 7-3), cleanout. Same as flushing inlet (F.I.). Provides access from the surface to flush out sewer lines.

concentric, having the same center.

condominium, complex of residential or office units which can be owned by individuals. Each unit carries a proportionate undivided ownership in the underlying real property.

conduit, pipe or tube for conveying fluid, or a structure containing ducts.

contour (Figs. 5-6 and 5-7), line joining points of equal elevation.

contour grading (Fig. 5-14), method of design using proposed finished contours. May be used for determination of earthwork (Fig. 5-16).

corporation cock, valve for controlling the flow of fluid or gas from a main to a customer (also called corporation stop).

cos, cosine, ratio (in a triangle with one angle of 90°) of the length of the side next to the angle divided by the length of the hypotenuse.

crest vertical curve (Fig. 6-9), continuously bending line that provides a smooth change from a positive to a negative slope, from a positive to a flatter positive slope, and from a negative to a steeper negative slope.

cross section (Fig. 2-16), plane that cuts through at right angles to the horizontal. Also refers to a drawing of this plane.

crown, highest point in the cross section of a street—usually at the center.

CSP, corrugated steel pipe.

CTB, cement-treated base.

curb return, curved section connecting curbs at intersecting streets.

D

daylight, term used in earthwork to designate the point at which a cut slope meets natural ground. Also to daylight. To cut or fill to natural ground.

development plan, plan prepared for the use of the developer. It shows lots with building footprints (outlines) and any additional information that will be useful, e.g., house plan designation and exterior finishes, plan for finished grading, indication of setback distances for zoning, locations of driveways, water, gas, and sewer laterals and mailboxes.

DIP, ductile iron pipe. Used where extra compressive strength is needed because of shallowness, or where tensile strength is needed for a pressure system.

drainage basin (Fig. 8-2), area that contributes storm water to a particular waterway.

drainage release point (Fig. 6-13), horizontal and vertical location where drainage is released from one drainage basin into the next.

dry well, hole dug in the ground which is then filled with aggregate to provide small capacity underground storage of drainage until water can percolate into the ground.

E

easement, right held by one owner for a specific use of the land of another. Also the location or description of that right.

effluent, fluid that flows out.

E.I.T., engineer in training. Term given to the first half of the professional license examination for engineers. Also, a person who has passed the E.I.T. examination.

ER (Fig. 6-14), end of return. The BC or EC of a curb at connecting streets.

event, storm, e.g., a storm of an intensity so great that it occurs only once every 100 years is sometimes called a 100-year *event*. This terminology is used for other return periods as well.

EWL, equivalent wheel loads.

F

fault, fracture of the earth's crust where slippage has occurred either horizontally or vertically.

fault zone, area on either side of an earthquake fault to be kept clear of structures because of the risk of earthquake damage.

FF, finished floor. Usually accompanied by the elevation thereof. Found on architectural and grading plans.

FGI, flat grate inlet.

FI (Fig. 8-7*a*), field inlet. A storm water inlet, whose top usually has an open grate.

F.I. (Fig. 7-3), Flushing inlet. A sanitary sewer connection to allow cleanout of a line. Same as CO (cleanout).

flow line, path traced by liquid. Usually along the invert of a pipe line or ditch.

flow rate, quantity of fluid passing a point in time, e.g., cubic feet per second (cfs), million gallons per day (million gpd or mgd).

footprint, outline of a building.

force flow, liquid moved through a conduit under pressure.

force main, utility conduit carrying flow under pressure rather than by the force of gravity.

fps, feet per second.

freeboard, distance between the water level and the top edge of the ditch or the top of the pipe.

french curve, flat drafting template of scroll-like curves. Used to draw curves of varying radii.
French drain, drainage ditch filled with aggregate.

G

gpd/cap, gallons per day per capita.
gravity flow, flow of liquid drawn through a conduit or along a channel by the force of gravity.
grid paper, drafting paper on which a grid is printed to facilitate plotting of cross sections.
guinea, 2×2 wooden hub used by surveyors as a vertical reference point.
guinea hopper, construction worker who reads information from survey stakes and calls it out to the equipment operator.
GV, gate valve.

H

ha, hectare or hectares. One hectare $= 10{,}000 \text{ m}^2 = 2.47$ acres.
hard copy, used to mean a variety of things by different individuals. Usually a drawing ready for a drafter. Often the culmination of several alternative designs.
Hardy-Cross solution, method using systematic, successive corrections for assumed flows in a piping system. Used to design water supply networks.
head loss, loss of pressure, often due to friction or turbulence caused by bends and changes in a piping or channel system.
hectare, metric unit for measurement of area of land, abbreviated ha. One hectare $= 100$ ares $= 10{,}000 \text{ m}^2 = 2.47$ acres.
HGL (Fig. 8-18), hydraulic grade line.
HI, height of instrument. Surveying term that indicates the elevation at the line of sight on a transit or level.
hinge point (HP) (Fig. 5-9), location where the slope of a cross section changes—usually at the start of a cut or fill slope.
hydraulic grade line (Fig. 8-18), a line to which the water level would rise in a vertical tube above conduit under pressure.
hydraulic radius (R_H) (Fig. 7-2),

$$R_H = \frac{a}{p} = \frac{\text{cross-sectional area}}{\text{wetted perimeter}}$$

hydraulics, science of the mechanics of fluids at rest and in motion.
hydrograph, drawing of the water level or rate of flow plotted against time.
hydrology, science of the natural occurrence, distribution, and circulation of water on the earth and in the atmosphere.
hypotenuse, longest side in a right (90°) triangle. The side opposite the 90° angle.

I

IDF chart (Fig. 8-1), graph of intensity, duration, and frequency.
impermeable, not permitting passage of fluid.
interpolate, process for estimating an intermediate term.
interstices, spaces between parts, e.g., the spaces between the rocks in a layer of aggregate.
invert, inside bottom of the pipe. The flow line.
iterate, to do repeatedly.

J

jurisdiction, power or authority over particular areas, i.e., the city, county, a flood control district, a sanitation district, etc.

K

key, keylock, groove or berm formed in material (concrete, earth, wood) to be fitted with a corresponding berm or groove on the matching layer to prevent slippage.

L

lateral, pipe connecting a utility main with facilities at the sides.
liquefaction, process of liquifying.
looping, technique of connecting conduits so that few or no dead-end branches of piping exist.
L.S., licensed surveyor.
L.S.I.T., licensed surveyor in training. First half of the examination for surveyor's license. Also a person who has passed the L.S.I.T. examination.
LTB, lime-treated base.

M

main, primary branch of a piping system.
Manning's equation,

$$V = \frac{1.486}{n} R_H^{2/3} S^{1/2}$$

where V = velocity, fps
n = coefficient of friction
R_H = wetted perimeter, feet
S = slope in feet per 100 ft

map, 1. plan view illustration usually drawn to scale to represent the relative locations of property and streets. 2. legal document to establish property exactly.
microfiche, photographic copy of maps or other documents in a form suitable for filing.
mobilization, assembling equipment and personnel into readiness for some activity.
mylar, polyester, filmlike material for drafting or printing reproducible copies.

N

NCPI, National Clay Pipe Institute.

O

off-site, areas or facilities outside of the property lines or boundaries of a project.
on-site, areas or facilities within the property lines or boundaries of a project.
order of magnitude, relative size of a number.
outfall, place where a sewer line discharges.
overfill, 1. placing material beyond the required area, horizontally. Usually to facilitate the use of equipment. 2. Placing material deeper than required in order to promote compaction.
overt, inside top of the pipe.

P

parabolic curve, 1. curve used to form smooth transitions for vertical changes of directions for streets and pipes. 2. curve formed by the intersection of a right circular cone with a plane parallel with the side.
parcel map, map prepared to divide property into a limited number of units.

patio home, private residence which is placed along one property side line so that there is a usable side yard on the opposite side. The side of the house placed on the property line has no windows or doors.

PCC, portland cement concrete. Concrete made with portland cement as designated by ASTM.

P.E., professional engineer. Person who has passed a licensing examination for engineers.

peak flow, maximum instantaneous flow.

peaking factor, multiplier to be applied to an average flow to yield a maximum instantaneous or peak flow.

percolate, to pass through a porous material.

percolation pond, small body of water held to facilitate seepage into the groundwater reservoir.

perforated pipe, conduit with holes to allow groundwater to seep into the pipe so that it may be transported to a drainage system.

permeable, capable of being penetrated through pores.

PI, point of intersection.

plan, design or list of steps to accomplish some task. Usually drawings made to scale showing necessary information for construction of structures.

planimeter (Fig. 5-10), instrument for measuring areas.

planned development, project put together to provide amenities in a creative way.

plasticity, quality of being capable of being molded or shaped.

PMP, perforated metal pipe. Used to collect and drain underground water.

PMS, plant-mixed surfacing. Asphaltic material mixed at a central plant to be placed as roadway or for parking surfaces.

POC, point on curve.

point of concentration, location where drainage comes together, e.g., storm water inlet.

POT, point on tangent.

PRC, point of reverse curvature.

profile (Fig. 2-16), line representing a longitudinal, vertical section through a roadway or pipeline.

profile paper, drafting paper with a grid printed on it to facilitate plotting.

PS, protective slope. Usually accompanied by the elevation at the highest elevation on a building foundation for earth.

PVC, polyvinyl chloride pipe.

Pythagorean theorem,

$$h^2 = a^2 + b^2$$

where h = the hypotenuse or longest side in a 90° triangle.
a = one leg adjacent ot the right angle of a right triangle.
b = leg adjacent to the right angle of a right triangle.

Q

Q, quantity of flow. Usually in cubic feet per second (cfs) or million gallons per day (million gpd or mgd).

R

rational formula,

$$Q = CIA$$

where Q = quantity of runoff, cfs
C = runoff coefficient
I = rainfall intensity, in/h
A = area, acres

RCP, reinforced concrete pipe.

R.C.E. registered civil engineer. A person who has passed the licensing examination for civil engineers.

R.E., 1. registered engineer. A person who has passed the licensing examination for engineers. 2. resident engineer. A person stationed at the job site to ensure that the work is performed according to the plans and specifications.

release point (Fig. 6-13), horizontal and vertical location where drainage is released from one drainage basin into the next.

retention pond, basin to hold storm water runoff and to provide a gradual release of it through the drainage facilities.

return period, amount of time between storms of a particular intensity.

R_H (Fig. 7-2), hydraulic radius,

$$R_H = \frac{a}{p} = \frac{\text{cross-sectional area}}{\text{wetted perimeter}}$$

right-of-way, strip of property provided for a street, highway, or other public facility.

runoff coefficient (c), number representing the amount of water running off an area as a proportion of the amount falling on it—based on type of soil, coverage, and evenness and degree of slope.

S

sag vertical curve (Fig. 6-9), continuously bending line that provides a smooth change from a negative to a positive slope, from a negative to a flatter negative slope, or from a positive to a steeper positive slope.

scale, 1. measuring stick. On an engineer's scale 1 in is divided into increments of 10, 20, 30, 40, 50, 60, or 80. On an architect's scale 1 in is divided into ½, ¼, ⅛, ¹⁄₁₆, ¹⁄₃₂, ³⁄₃₂. 2. to measure using a scale.

screening, 1. to cause material to pass through screens. A method for segregating sand and aggregate by size. 2. photographic procedure to give faded lines.

septic tank, underground holding tank to allow organic sewage to separate and decompose. It is connected to leach lines that draw off the purified liquid for percolation into the soil. Used for residences or other buildings where there is little sewage and no public sanitation facilities.

sewage, waterborne waste carried in sewers.

sewerage, network of sewer lines.

sheet flow, flow of liquid moving evenly over an area without being concentrated in swales.

significant figures, all the nonzero digits of a number and zeros at the end that show degree of precision (also significant digits).

sine, sin, ratio (in a triangle with one angle of 90°) of the length of the side opposite the angle divided by the length of hypotenuse.

slope (Fig. 5-1), degree of rise or fall of a line with reference to the vertical and horizontal plane.

SOP, standard operating procedure.

spread sheet (Fig. 11-1), chart for comparing the unit cost, item total cost, and project total cost of several proposals.

standpipe (Fig. 3-6), vertically mounted pipe open at the top with or without an elbow.

station, designation on a centerline or reference line at 100-ft intervals.

subdivision, parcel of land divided into lots for legal descriptions and real estate transactions.

subgrade, material placed below the surface to provide foundation for some structure.

subsidence, settling of the earth's surface sometimes due to excessive removal of groundwater.

superelevation, tilting of the cross slope of a roadbed to remove drainage, or on a curve, to compensate for centrifugal force.

swale, small valley area between two hills or mounds which is lower at one end. The swale provides a pathway for drainage.

SWE, Society of Women Engineers, United Engineering Center, 345 East 47th Street, New York, NY 10017.

SWI (Fig. 8-7), storm water inlet. Includes catch basins and field inlets.

T

tangent, 1. straight line or flat plane that touches a curve at a single point. The line or plane will be perpendicular to a radial line at that point. 2. tan. The ratio (in a triangle with one angle of 90°) of the length of the side opposite divided by the side adjacent.

TBM, temporary bench mark. See bench mark.

t_c, time of concentration.

TC, top of the curb.

topo, topography, physical features and relief of a site. Includes buildings, trees, utilities, paved areas, waterways, and elevations.

town house, single-family residential house which is attached to adjacent houses. The building includes ownership of underlying property.

tract map, map of a subdivision given a tract number to facilitate referencing.

Transite pipe, Johns-Manville Transite pipe is an asbestos-cement product.

traverse, path usually described with distances and bearings going from point to point or around a parcel of land.

trench spoil, earth dug out of a trench.

triangulations, technique for determining distances between points and verifying locations of points.

truncate, to cut off. A number will be truncated after the necessary number of significant figures.

TS, top of slab. Usually accompanied by the elevation thereof. Found on architectural, grading, and development plans.

U

UBC, Uniform Building Code, manual of specifications for building design.

undercut, excavating less in a horizontal direction than is called for. Usually done at property line or next to building pad.

UPC, Uniform Plumbing Code, manual used for plumbing specifications.

USC & GS, United States Coast and Geodetic Survey.

USGS, United States Geological Survey.

V

valley gutter (Figs. 6-22 and 8-9), concrete swale down the center of a street or across a secondary street.

VCP, vitrified clay pipe. Usually used for sanitary sewers with less than a 42-in diameter.

vellum, high quality, translucent drafting paper.

W

w/, with

weighted average (Example 8-1), average value based on relative significance of the items being averaged.

wet well, chamber that fills to a designated level with fluid. At that level a pump is activated.

wetted perimeter, length, measured on the cross section, that will be wet when flowing at a designated depth.

wye, Y-shaped connector of pipes.

Index

Page numbers in *italic* indicate illustrations.

213